The Scratch of the Hop

The *Scratch* of the *Hop*

Hop picking in Herefordshire, Worcestershire & Shropshire

MARSHA O'MAHONY

LOGASTON PRESS

FRONT COVER, CLOCKWISE FROM TOP LEFT: Early twentieth-century photograph of hop pickers arriving by traction engine at Stoke Edith (© Derek Foxton); Hopyard at Instone Court, Bishops Frome (© Laura Haworth); Hops (© Markus Spiske); Lorry laden with hop pockets, c.1940s (© Brian Willder); A pair of round hop kilns near Mathon (© Philip Halling, Geograph); Busheller and hop pickers in a hopyard, c.1940s (© Brian Willder). FRONT FLAP: Young hop picker (© Miss White). BACK COVER: Hop kilns at Cradley (© Miss Wight). BACK FLAP: Marsha O'Mahony and Adrian Toma hop drying at Instone Court (both © Laura Haworth). FRONTISPIECE: Hop picking in Herefordshire in 1977 (© Derek Evans/ HARC).

First published in 2021 by Logaston Press
The Holme, Church Road, Eardisley HR3 6NJ
www.logastonpress.co.uk
An imprint of Fircone Books Ltd.

ISBN 978-1-910839-44-7

Designed and typeset by Richard Wheeler in 10 on 15 Baskerville.
Cover design by Richard Wheeler.

Printed and bound in Poland.

Logaston Press is committed to a sustainable future for our business, our readers and our planet.
The book in your hands is made from paper certified by the Forest Stewardship Council.

British Library Catalogue in Publishing Data.
A CIP catalogue record for this book is available from the British Library.

CONTENTS

Simon Parker of Instone Court, with a pocket of Admiral hops (© Laura Haworth)

FOREWORD

The challenge of growing hops is probably why I am still growing them. Like any perennial crop, you grow as much for next season as this one. Combined with the aroma at picking time, hop growing can be very addictive.

Unfortunately, hops are now a minority but specialist crop. In its heyday we were the second-largest grower in the world. Today we are seventh, with just 1.6% of the world market. Not only has a wealth of experience been lost, but also a unique social activity. The advent of machine harvesting in the sixties replaced the thousands of people travelling from the cities to pick by hand. We are now at a point where we are losing the generation that did the hand-picking.

The hop-growing season starts in March with stringing the new crop, and culminates in September with harvesting. The 50 or so individual hop growers left, who make up the membership of The British Hop Association (BHA), clear their diaries in September for their busiest time. We are lucky in this country to have the wealth of varieties in our breeding programme. This national collection of plants is the bedrock to the science behind the breeding.

I am a third-generation hop grower here at Instone near Bromyard and we are still growing hops in the same field my grandfather did. I have been lucky enough to be born into this way of life. I have always said, if I wasn't hop growing I would struggle to stay farming. I hope, after reading this book, people will appreciate the expertise, knowledge and sheer effort that goes into bringing you the ingredients for your English hopped beer. *Cheers!*

Simon Parker, Instone Court
(Chairman of British Hops Association)

Herefordshire hop picker, mid twentieth century (© Miss White)

ACKNOWLEDGEMENTS

I am indebted to those who contributed their personal experiences, who are listed, with gratitude, in the index. I have been welcomed into peoples' homes, farms, kilns, kitchens, supplied with copious cups of tea and fruit cake. It's been a joy. This has been an ever-expanding book, with the list of people to talk to getting longer each day. If I didn't reach you, forgive me – I would still love to hear your stories. With special thanks to: Bill Laws for his support and editing, and further editorial support from Logaston's Richard and Su Wheeler and for seeing the project off the ground. Thanks to Kate Bower, Di Everett, Laura O'Mahony, Sean O'Mahony and Andy Tatchell for their generosity, copious reading of copy and archive nous; Herefordshire Lore and its outstanding archive of first-hand accounts; to Simon Parker, hop grower at Instone Court; Charlie Pudge of Frogend Farm; Derek Foxton for kind use of his collection; Maureen Beauchamp for photos from her late father, Tony Williams' collection; John Symonds for illustrating the workings of a kiln; to Rhys Griffiths and the Herefordshire Archive and Records Centre (HARC); Steve Jones of Herefordshire Histories and the Herefordshire Museum and Libraries Service; Leominster Museum; John Pudge and the Hop Pocket & Hop Museum; Jonathan Blackman Hutchinsons Crop Protection Specialists; Will Kirby for his Bruff catalogue; Stoke Lacy History Project; Herefordshire Life Through a Lens & Catcher Media; Vernon and Peter Amor, Wye Valley Brewery; Gill Bullock, Swan Brewery; Peter Walker and the Bromyard and District Society; Herefordshire Women's Institute; Museum of Royal Worcester; Black Country Living Museum; Guinness Storehouse, Dublin; Kidderminster Carpet Museum; The Hive,

Worcester; Tom Nellist and the Trumpet & District Agricultural Society; the Ledbury Ploughing Society; master brewer Roger Putman; Heather Hurley and the Landscape Origins of the Wye project; Paul Corbett and Will Rogers of Charles Faram & Co. Ltd; Edward Lewis; James Sufton; Martin Griffiths; Carol Hall; June Gwynne; Peter Green; Derek Badham; Hellens House Archive; Clare Wichbold; Chris Over; Susannah Garland; Laura McCrae; Maddy Warhurst; Pauline Andrews; Pearl Griffiths; Ricky Ravenhill; Roger Baker; Sally Nunn; Reginald Gaunt; Steve Wright; Neil Wright; Andrew Lowe; Bev Wearire; Edie Pound; Hazel Parkinson; Helen Hughes; Jessie Dallow; Barbara Parkinson; Vera Hadley; George Hill; Sue Rice; Mark Andrews; Tom Probert; the Spilsbury family; John Walker; Robert Denny; Janet Brodie Murphy; Dorothy Masters; Jessie Watkins; Pearl Jeynes; Barbara Andrews; Roger Bray; Facebook Old Ledbury; Facebook Leominster Childhood Memories; Facebook Tenbury; The John Moore Society; Society of Independent Brewers (SIBA); Richard Blair and Jeremy Wikeley at the George Orwell Foundation; Herefordshire CAMRA; Brewing History Society; Sally Bevan; Robert Jones; Robert Hancocks, Wyercroft Farm and Susan Vaughan; Peter Cotton and Sally Pearson; Robin Peers and Robert Chapman; Philip Bowler, Frome Valley Transport; and Robert Simpson of Chicory Crops, who always encouraged me.

Marsha O'Mahony

This book is dedicated to the stoic band of West Midlands hop growers:
S.J. Adams & Son; M. & L. Andrews; Brook House Hops;
M., R. & A. Capper; H.J. Davies & Sons; P. & E. Edmondson;
R.J. & H.L. Hancocks; Hawkins Farming Partnership; J.S. &
C.P. Hawkins; E.R. Lane & Sons; E.L. Lewis & Son; T. Lewis;
Lupofresh Ltd Stockton Court; T.R. Morris & Son; Okells Organics;
S.J. Parker; H.G. Pennington & Sons; R.B. Phillips & Sons; G.W. &
E.A. Powell-Tuck; J.M. Probert & Son; C. J. Pudge; Farmer Pudge
& Co.; J.C. Pudge; T. Spilsbury; J. & T. Walker and F. Young.

1

The Hop Story

*There can be little doubt that the industry which is most prosperous in
Worcestershire today, and especially in the Valley of the Teme and its tributaries,
is that of hop growing. Indeed, the same may be said of Herefordshire, where
I had the pleasure of meeting a gentleman who is reported to have realised a
considerable fortune, and to have purchased an estate out of the profits earned by
him in this industry.*

H. Rider Haggard, *Rural England Volume 1,* 1902

NEWCOMERS to the hop-growing areas of Herefordshire, Shropshire and
Worcestershire may wonder about the strange goings-on behind tall
hedges and poplar trees. Tantalising glimpses reveal a canopy of tall structures, held together with crocheted, zig-zag patterns of string and wire, up
which grow a green perennial, vine-like plant. As harvest time approaches
the hopyard sings and whistles as the wind breezes through the trellis, hop
cones dripping lightly from the end of the bines. The aroma will hit you
first, at the back of the throat: strong, punchy. It's not unpleasant. Nearby,
scattered around, are square, sometimes round, redbrick buildings, a white
spinning cowl on top; these are the cook-houses or the kilns, the engine
rooms of the hop farm, where the magic happens. Today all this passes with
barely a mention. Except, that is, to an exclusive group: those who have been
'scratched by the hop'.

The hop *(Humulus lupulus)* is a tough, scratchy, prickly plant that is the
essential constituent of beer, adding a distinctive bitterness. In a pint glass,
the hop 'juice' becomes cool, smooth, earthy, sweet, spicy, the tastes of the
countryside. Botanists attest to its unique nature: it is related to the cannabis
plant (with none of its effects; they belong to the same botanical family – the

cannabaceae); grows on a complex grid of wire and string, reaching up to 5.5 metres; its roots can live and thrive to a great age, but it is subject to some ruinous pests and diseases. So much can go wrong during the growing process. It is a crop that induces headache and heartache, and joy and jubilation unlike any other. Why does the grower bother? Because this is a plant that reaches parts others don't. It touches the heart and the soul. It appeals to all the senses – touch, smell and taste. It is the central ingredient of beer, the elixir of the brew. The contents of your pint glass have a far richer history than you can imagine. The impression of the hop remains seared on the memory, long after others have come and gone.

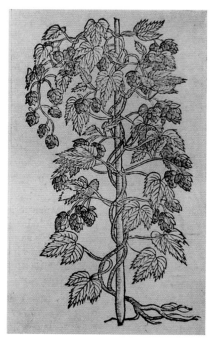

1581 woodcut of the hop by C. Plantin

Its allure and magic are part of folklore. But its position in the region's social history does not make it a heritage industry, set in aspic, forever to be admired from afar. It is living and breathing and can, when the circumstances are right, be a formidable economic beast, with bountiful profits. Other times it can cripple the grower. There have been huge changes in the industry. In the 1880s there were around 74,000 growers in the UK across 54 counties, as far north as Aberdeen. By 1958 these had fallen to 2,600. In 2020, this number had been further reduced to around just 50, and of these, a hardy and indomitable 23 farmers hold their nerve, and continue to raise this crop in the West Midlands.

The natural environment – the *terroir* – of this area is different to that of its closest hop neighbours in the south-east, though it would take a highly attuned palette to detect it. Here it is clay soil, deep and rich, offering distinct growing conditions, producing a range of flavours that cannot be matched anywhere else in the world. The West Midlands is the most northerly outpost of the world's hop-growing areas and our maritime climate further adds to its distinctiveness.

Hops growing at Instone Court, near Bromyard (© Laura Haworth)

The hop produces a cone, a series of delicate scales, at the base of which is a sticky yellowish, golden powder, lupulin, containing oils and resins. Hop lupulin is unique in the plant world, eminently suitable for brewing beer as well as some healing purposes. These are the brewer's precious commodities, the frankincense and myrrh they use to brew the signature bitter taste so emblematic of British beer.

Daniel Defoe saw much to interest him on his perambulation of Herefordshire and Worcestershire in 1724, and encountered wildly contrasting scenes to those he described in his *Robinson Crusoe*, but no less exotic. His observations were among the first to reference hop growing in the West Midlands, bringing the activity to a wider audience. A century or so later, growers here were beginning to build a reputation for their innovation, and they have continued that spirit of improvement well into the twenty-first century. It was here, in the nineteenth century, that quality aroma hops were adopted (far earlier than their counterparts in the south-east), and developments in cultivation, mechanisation and drying drew the attention of West Midlands growers too.

In his 1958 novel, *September Moon*, the writer John Moore wrote an affectionate tribute to the hop, a paean to typical harvesting scenes played out across hop-growing districts:

Hop picking at Dormington in 1948 (© Tony Williams, Derek Foxton Archive)

Hop picking was indeed a kind of a play acted for a month in this amphitheatre that lay between the Malverns and the Welsh Hills. The hop pickers provided the chorus; miners on holidays from Wales, factory workers from the Midlands, Gypsies, all thrown together against the green frieze of the hops under the sun.

The spectacle of the harvest, representing a cross-section of humanity brought together by the hop, has become almost mythical. In the middle of the last century, hop was king. Most farms in the West Midlands grew them, from just a few acres to hundreds. It was worth their while; good money could be earned. They provided a valuable additional source of revenue, fitting well into a farming system of livestock, fruit, crops for feed and dung from livestock for the hopyards. But this mercurial crop was also sometimes blamed for distracting the farmer from more certain and reliable lines of production.

Its stamp on the countryside was distinctive: orderly rows, sturdy wirework supporting beautifully-strung hopyards stretching as far as the eye could see. Harvest-time attracted thousands of hand-pickers from across the Midlands, Liverpool, Manchester, Bath, Bristol, South Wales and London; and Gypsies in their caravans, arriving on foot, bicycle, tandem, horse and cart, truck, char-abanc, coach, train and, on at least one occasion, boat – an exodus of a labour force often unremarked upon. Their appearance transformed hitherto sleepy, rural communities into hives of often frenzied and noisy activity, the like of which has not been seen since. It was a movement of people unprecedented outside of war time or pandemic. Their arrival ensured the hop was picked, but not without a fair dose of drama. There was singing, dancing, fighting, horse-dealing, romances, births, drinking, scrumping, deaths, marriages, poaching, holidaying and far more besides. Despite all of this, the harvest always came in. It had to. There was an awful lot resting on it for the grower.

Gypsy child, Rosie Butler (daughter of Pearly Butler) making mud pies in the hopyard at Claston Farm, Dormington, 1957 (© Derek Evans/ HARC)

A lesson where and when to plant
good Hopyard

Whome fancie persuadeth, among other crops,
  to have for his spending, sufficient of hops,
Must willinglie follow, of choises to chuse,
  such lessons approved, as skilfull doo use.

Ground gravellie, sandie, and mixed with clay,
  is naughtie for hops any maner of way;
Or if it be mingled with rubbish and stone,
  for drines and barrenness, let it alone.

Choose soile for the hop of the rottenest mould,
  well doonged and wrought, as a garden plot should:
Not far from the water (but not overflowne)
  this lesson well noted is meete to be knowne.

The Sunne in the south, or else southly and west,
  is joy to the hop, as a welcomed gest;
But wind in the north, or else northly east,
  to hop is as ill as a fraie in a feast.

Meete plot for a hopyard once found is as told,
  make thereof account, as of jewell of gold.
Now dig it and leave it, the Sunne for to burne,
  and afterward fence it, to serve for that turne.

The hop for his profit I thus doo exalt,
  it strengtheneth drinke, and it favoreth malt.
And being well brewed, long kept it will last,
  And drawing abide, if ye drawe not too fast.

Thomas Tusser, *Five Hundred Pointes of Good Husbandrie*, 1557

For all its close associations with an English identity, the hop is not a native plant. It arrived from Flanders in 1525, carried by refugees fleeing religious persecution. They, with their inherent growing knowledge of this challenging crop, came to monopolise hop growing for several decades. English growers struggled to adopt it, and became reliant on their Flemish neighbours' expertise. But this changed in 1574 when the godfather of English hop growing, Reynolde Scot, set out to reform hop cultivation with his book, *A Perfite Platforme of a Hoppe Garden*. Rather like William Tyndale, whose translation of the Bible into English (also in the sixteenth century) made it accessible to all, Scot's work did something similar for illiterate farmers, demystifying hop husbandry through a series of woodblock illustrations. Here on in, the hop's hold on the English countryside, farming, our taste buds and psyche, had begun.

By the 1800s commercial hop growing was expanding, centred largely in the West Midlands and Kent areas. The availability of huge labour populations from industrial centres nearby (Birmingham, the Black Country and south Wales in the case of the West Midlands) was significant. By the beginning of the twentieth century the status of the hop in English culture,

Hop workers posing in a hopyard, with a wagon loaded with hops in green sacks, c.1930
(© Mr and Mrs Gilbert/ Herefordshire Lore)

Hops ripening on the bine (© Markus Spiske)

commerce and economics had been firmly planted. Even interfering with a hop plant became a crime, as one poor gentleman found to his cost.

In the *Worcestershire Chronicle* of October 1901, George Price, 46, was indicted for unlawfully cutting down 76 hop bines, the property of Mr Herbert Adams at Knighton-on-Teme. His actions were not mere vandalism, but something altogether more serious: he had committed an offence against the realm. Under an Act of George IV, the cutting of hop bines (growing up poles) was made a statutory offence, a clear indication, if ever one was needed, of its value and importance to the West Midlands' economy and the national one too. The Chairman of the bench described Price's actions as, 'very much a serious offence, I wish the power to flog was not confined to youthful offenders, but to you too! This prisoner deserves to be severely punished.' Price was duly sentenced to six months' hard labour. The message was clear: do not mess with hops!

Today, growers, pickers, marketeers and brewers continue to battle with the hop's mercurial nature. There have been tough times, and there have been good times, but this is a crop, a people, a business and an industry, digging deep and focussing on the future.

These are their extraordinary stories.

2

Celebrating the Hop

THE seductive magic of the hop has inspired generations of growers, pickers and interested passers-by, to song, music, poetry, prose, literature and art. Theirs is often a curious and romantic response to a plant that continues to befuddle, tax and challenge the grower. But that is the effect of the hop on you. Its celebration has been both sophisticated and naïve, honest and embellished, serving as a reminder of the power it once held on the collective memory and personal testimony.

HOPS IN PROSE

Over the centuries the famous and the non-famous alike, unencumbered by the scientific, botanic or economic, have fallen sway to its lyrical nature. The love affair has not been as ardent for some, however. Daniel Defoe's observations on his tour of Herefordshire in 1724 were not so flattering, particularly in Ross-on-Wye. Here he encountered some, 'good cider and a good trade on the River Wye, and nothing else as I remember, except for a monstrous fat woman!' He described the populace of the area as:

> a diligent and laborious people, chiefly addicted to husbandry and they boast they have the finest wool, the best and the richest cyder in all Britain. As for hops, they plant in abundance, indeed all over this county, and they are very good.

A century and a half later and another writer of adventure stories with exotic themes arrived in the area with a serious purpose in mind. H. Rider Haggard (1856–1925), best known for *King Solomon's Mines,* was also an agricultural reformist. He was on a research mission across rural England to explore

Hop pickers at Newton Dilwyn, 1903. A posed photograph by Alfred Watkins, with tally-man (see p. 110) behind the crib to the left and the busheller to his right (© Hereford Libraries)

agricultural conditions and economy. His prodigious notes were reproduced in his volumes, *Rural England,* in 1902, which won wide respect. Delivered in straight reportage with little literary flourish, they contained some prescient observations that resonate with today's growers:

> Labour is becoming scarcer and scarcer. I find it impossible, considering the county as a whole, to prophesy smooth things of the future of agriculture in Herefordshire. I am driven to say that the outlook looks black in this beautiful and fertile land. Still, there are bright spots on the horizon. I refer especially to the remunerative culture of fruit and hops.

What I have most wanted to do … is to make political writing into an art.
George Orwell, *Why I Write*, 1946

There were no rose-coloured spectacles for George Orwell when it came to hop picking. He cut through the romance and painted a pretty grim picture of the industry in Kent in 1931 in his essay for the *New Statesman and Nation*. He later went on to fictionalise his experiences in his 1935 novel, *A Clergyman's Daughter*. In his *Diaries* he complained about the hop's roughness and how it stained his hands – a common complaint that was, for the most part, endured by many pickers. Others who could afford it, bought gloves. For Orwell though:

> One's hands get stained black (...) with the hop-juice, which only mud will remove, and after a day or two they crack and are cut to bits by the stems of the vines, which are spiny. In the mornings, before the cuts had reopened, my hands used to give me perfect agony. It wasn't a bad life, but what with standing all day, sleeping rough and getting my hands cut to bits, I felt a wreck at the end of it. It was humiliating to see that most of the people there looked on it as a holiday – in fact, it is because hopping is regarded as a holiday that pickers will take such starvation wages. It gives one an insight into the lives of farm labourers, too, to realise that, according to their standards, hop picking is hardly work at all.

George Orwell's son, Richard Blair, has happier memories of hop picking:

> My experience of hop picking was back in the early '60s on a very large 1,100-acre arable farm spread between Westhide and Woodmanton [Herefordshire] on the Hereford–Worcester road, where they grew about a 100 hop-acres of Fuggles and Brewer hops. My involvement was relatively minor as I was essentially their main tractor driver/ ploughman, with relief milking, but I did all the fertilizer spreading, inter-row cultivations, a (very) little stringing and setting the bines onto the strings (tedious) and some harvesting when all the hop pickers had gone off back to Birmingham on Thursdays to "sign on" for their unemployment benefit! September was geared to hops and all else fell by the wayside! But nevertheless it was great experience, and the smell of a hop is very evocative. I was there for four years from '64 to '68.

John Moore (1909–67) was part of the great Edwardian generation of English writers, whose contemporaries included the likes of Evelyn Waugh, John Betjeman, Daphne du Maurier, H.E. Bates and the aforementioned George Orwell. Moore had a varied career. A veteran correspondent of the Spanish Civil War, he was also a founder and driving force behind the Cheltenham Literary Festival (1949). He also wrote the script for a 1957 film, *The England of Elizabeth*, with a score composed by Ralph Vaughan Williams. But it is for his 1958 novel *September Moon* that he is most widely known in hop growing circles. Set in

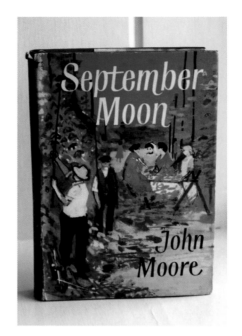

September Moon by John Moore

the hop growing areas of Herefordshire, the action takes place in the month of September, the picking season. It features a host of familiar characters from the Welsh Valleys, the Black Country, Herefordshire and the Gypsy community. Against the backdrop of the harvest, it is the story of two lovers, Tim Sollars and Marianne Tomkins. They come from antagonistic families, the *Capulets* and the *Montagues* of the hopyards, both battling for supremacy. Their feud is paralleled in a sub-plot around two Gypsy families headed by Wisdom Lee, King of the Gypsies, and his rival Black Barty. There is no record of Moore's visit to the area (most likely Bishops Frome) but he must have spent time there for he knew his subject, the area and the industry well. We do have one solitary connection worth recording and it is a story told to Charles Pudge, hop grower at Frogend, Bishops Frome:

> Black Barty in *September Moon* was based on Black Harry, who was an infamous Gypsy. His daughter lived next to us at one time. He used to get on very well with my father and they never crossed swords or anything.

You never want to go east of the Malverns, it's horrible over there.
Geoffrey Bright, *West of the Malverns,* 1948

On June 6, 1918, a young Lieutenant Geoffrey Bright found himself an unexpected hero. As the most junior officer of the 4th Battalion of the King's Shropshire Light Infantry, he led his depleted battalion in a charge to take a German post in Bligny, near Rheims, France. Facing a hail of machine-gun fire, he ignored all safety for himself. His actions led to promotion to Captain, and the award of the *Croix de Guerre avec Palme.* In the years following, he enjoyed multifarious success and respect as an auctioneer with Russell, Baldwin & Bright, and as a renowned antiques expert, and a writer and poet. His book of poems, *Hereford is Heaven,* is a creative sketch of the characters he encountered in the Herefordshire and Welsh border country, and his poem, *Hops,* evokes the picking season in ten verses, capturing all the elements of the extravaganza:

Geoffrey Bright (© Mark Adams)

When morning mists in autumn, weave patterns in the vale,
And heavy dews that hint at frost, the lush green meadows pale;
And sheaves of corn in barn and rick, declare the harvest home,
Men still have hops to gather, down by the River Frome.
From many a smoke-drenched city, from many a dreary slum,
From many a gaunt Welsh mining town, the pale-faced families come,
By train and bus to Ledbury Town, excited, noisy and gay
The happiest time in their drab lives – a holiday with pay.

Geoffrey Bright, *Hereford is Heaven,* 1948

It is possible that Bright encountered Raine Geoghegan's family in the Frome Valley. She is a Romany poet and author, some of her work harking back to the period when Bright was writing. She recorded the memories of her parents and grandparents and their stories inspired a collection of poetry and prose. Her Welsh father, a pole puller, and Gypsy mother, a picker, met in the hop fields of Bishops Frome in the 1950s, just one of hundreds of relationships and marriages that blossomed (while others floundered!) Based in Malvern today, Raine is close to the hop grounds of her parents' youth. Incorporating words from the Romany language, *Kamavtu* is an ode to her parents:

Kamavtu (*I love you*)

Mother was from Middlesex,
Father, the Welsh Valleys.
He was a pole puller, she picked hops.
One Friday night
under a sickle of moonlight
they sat on a bench
in front of the Green Dragon Pub.
The landlord had filled an old bath with beer,
the hoppers were dipping their mugs into the frothy liquid,
which dripped onto their bare chests.
They were smiling as they wiped their mouths on the backs of their arms.
Father and Mother sat quietly holding hands.
He leaned in close, was about to kiss her cheek
when a voice hollered from the darkness.
'Phylly, jel on, let's get back to the vardo.'
'It's me Dad,' she said.
She jumped up, straightening her long red skirt
then quickly turned and whispered,
'Kamavtu Jimmy.'
He didn't know many Romani words, but this one, well he just knew.

Above and left: Gypsy family, the Ripleys, who picked hops for the Pudges at Bishops Frome for several generations (© Raine Geoghegan)

Below: Gypsy camp at Malvern (© Miss White)

15

The famous children's novel *The Railway Children* (1906), and its later film adaptation, has been loved by generations of families. Its author, Edith Nesbit (1858–1924) had a turbulent personal life, living at different periods of her life in Kent and Sussex. It is perhaps where she was inspired by the hop fields nearby and penned this poem. There is a weariness to her words and a yearning too:

> Ah me, how pleasant to go down
> From the forlorn and faded town
> To Kentish wood and fold and lane,
> And breathe God's blessed air again;
> Where glorious yellow corn-fields blaze
> And nuts hang over woodland ways.
>
> To pick the sweet keen-scented hops,
> (See from each pole a dream-wreath drops)
> To toil all day in pure clear air,
> Laughter and sunshine everywhere,
> With reddening woods and sweet wet soil
> And well-earned rest and honest toil.

EXECUTION BALLAD

Fights, thieving, scrumping apples, all pale into insignificance when compared to murder. But The Homme hop farm, Weobley, was the location of a grisly crime in 1895. Hop pickers, Ann Dickson, with her toddler, and Mary Ann Farrell, were in Weobley for the picking season and were enjoying themselves in one of the village pubs after a day scratting, when they met John Hill, alias Sailor Jack, and John Williams, alias Irish Jack, also in the area for the harvest. After an evening drinking, the two women made their way back to their barracks, but were attacked, resulting in Ann's murder and Mary suffering a serious assault. The child was unharmed. Hill and Williams were found guilty of 'wilful murder' and in November 1885 were hanged at Hereford Gaol's first-ever private execution. The sad events were recorded in an execution ballad. The author is unknown:

The victim has been labouring,
In the hop gardens we're told,
When her work was over then,
Alas her life was sold,
She met with Williams and John Hill,
At a public in the town,
And before the dawn of early morn,
In death she was struck down.

EASELS AND PAINTBRUSHES — HOPS IN ART

Sir Alfred Munnings was an English Impressionist painter (1878–1959) and considered one of the finest painters of horses of his generation. He became fascinated by the Stevens and Loveday Gypsy families and their horse-drawn caravans as they followed the hop-picking season in the Hampshire countryside. These encounters inspired a series of work from the hopyards in the early 1900s. In his memoirs, *An Artist's Life* published in 1950, he wrote:

> Never in my life have I been so filled with a desire to work as I was then.
> Mrs Loveday posed in all her finery for this picture, holding a black
> horse. In the centre, Mark Stevens was harnessing a white horse to a blue
> Romany-looking, ship-shaped caravan. Children and dogs were in the
> foreground. What days! What models!

Munnings introduced another painter and kindred spirit to the characters that inhabited hopyards, Dame Laura Knight. She was a one-time resident of Malvern during the pre-Second World War years, and, like Munnings, her subjects included Gypsies, dancers and circus performers. Between 1911 and 1929, she painted some of the most famous ballet dancers of the day from Sergei Diaghilev's *Ballet Russes*, including ballerina Anna Pavlova. During the Second World War she was a member of the War Artists Advisory Committee, and in 1945 she recorded the trials of Nazi war criminals at Nuremberg in a series of portraits. It was a far, far cry from the quiet hum of hopyards under the shadow of the Malvern Hills, where she set her easel in 1937 at Maurice Averill's Callow End. She found much to interest her there, particularly Gypsy workers, and produced a number of works that hang in galleries and private collections today. In her autobiography, she wrote:

'Hop Picking' by Sir Alfred Munnings (© Sheffield Museums Trust)

At the door of the taxi which I hired daily to take me to Callow End, I always found an elderly man, named Godfrey, who was ready and waiting to go with me, despite my wish for his absence. He knew all about hops. He knew all about everything in this world as well as in the world to come … he knew all about art and artists, and what would make the best picture in a hop field. Like painting anything on the move, such as race-meeting crowds, the constant change taking place during the stripping of the hop vines is nervy work. An artist has to finish as he goes; you cannot reckon on seeing the same thing twice. One evening, I was trying to add last touches to a canvas, when I was roughly interrupted by a lot of Gypsies yelling at me, "that man of yours has got a badger he's bringing for you!"

The Magic of the Line, 1965

Margaret Stevens (Mrs Mark Stevens) in the doorway of her caravan. Munnings' hop-picking paintings featured members of the Stevens family of Romany Gypsies. The family picked for many years at the Pudges' farm at Bishops Frome. One of the members of the family painted by Munnings was Margaret Stevens, pictured above in later years (© the Stevens Family)

In a contemporary newspaper account, the matriarchal Gypsy, Gypsy Lee, who was the focus of Knight's work, was tracked down. The Lee family had been returning to Callow End for decades and were unimpressed by this scion of the art world. Gypsy Lee was interviewed, her age 'unknown or forgotten'. Barely looking up from her hands as she scratted the hops, she had only one thing to say: 'I should like to have seen the result.' It's unlikely she ever did.

Graduates of Hereford Art School, John Ward and Jehan Daly enjoyed a peaceful and stress-free autumn picking hops just before the outbreak of the Second World War. Ward is best known as the artist from whom the Prince of Wales received his first lessons in painting. Connections with the Royal Family continued over the course of his professional life, with an invitation to sketch family life at Balmoral; he was also a guest at the Prince of Wales's wedding to Lady Diana Spencer in 1981. His pencil drawings of that event later led to a painting of the occasion. In the late summer of 1939, Ward and his friend Daly were staying with Ward's parents in Church Street, within sight of Hereford Cathedral. Saddle-bags packed with spare clothes, sandwiches and flasked tea, they set out along country lanes aiming for hopyards near Ledbury, where they filled cribs for a day or two before leaving to join the Royal Engineers. They didn't earn lots, and it didn't seem to matter too much: 'we were much too slow compared to the locals and Gypsies.'

Royal Worcester 'Mathon' porcelain

It is perhaps not surprising that Royal Worcester should feature hops in their designs, with the district criss-crossed with hundreds of hopyards at one time. The Worcester hop pattern is named after a variety of hops grown in and around the village of the same name on the Worcestershire/ Herefordshire border: *Mathon*. The design was first used in around 1795 (during the Flight and Barr period), and was resurrected in 1955, with the foreman painter Harry Davis reworking the original paintings and drawings to create a pattern that would fit the various forms of the factory's porcelain. The pattern took about ten years to develop, and was finally introduced in 1966.

Singing to the hopyards, singing again on the way back home, around the camp-fire, around the crib, was all part of the hop picker's experience. There were the favourites and crowd-pleasers, *She'll be Coming 'Round the Mountain* was one, and *It's a Long Way to Tipperary* another, a chorus of voices, sometimes riotous, but good-natured, and, if they were lucky, accompanied by guitar, accordion or fiddle. Early in the twentieth century, a Radnorshire farming family diary records in careful copperplate how a Gypsy family, the Lockes, departed the valley for the picking seasons of potato, fruit and hops, leaving their mistress behind. As the caravans bump along the track leading out of the valley, the sounds of the fiddle, accordion and song accompanied their departure to the picking fields to the east.

Herefordshire folklorist, Ella Mary Leather, enjoyed similar impromptu concerts from the Locke family at her home, The Homme in Weobley, a hop-growing farm. She recognised early on the urgent need to record the folk customs, stories and songs of rural communities – the tunes and lyrics normally handed down through the oral tradition. Her knowledge of the countryside and its inhabitants, in particular the Gypsy community, led to a fruitful working relationship with Cecil Sharp, founding father of the folk song revival. On their research travels around the countryside, Leather and Sharp ensured this music would be saved for posterity by making wax cylinder recordings. Often travelling in an old dog cart, Leather noted down many tunes she heard on her travels. As Roy Palmer records:

> The singers were labourers, a blacksmith, a molecatcher's widow, servants and Gypsies. Mrs Leather even learned to pick hops – an extraordinary step for a middle-class lady of the time – so as to work alongside Gypsy women and gain first their confidence, then hear their songs.
>
> *The Folklore of Hereford and Worcester*, 1992

At the 1908 Three Choirs Festival, Leather was introduced to the composer, Ralph Vaughan Williams. It was to be a fruitful relationship. Between 1909 and 1913, he returned every year for hop picking and joined Leather in her forays across the hop-growing districts. It was on one of these that Leather records his first encounter with the Jones family at Monkland, Leominster, who were resting after a day's hop picking. You can almost feel the chill on

Gypsy family, the Butlers, gathered around the camp-fire at Claston, Dormington, in the 1950s
(© Derek Evans/ HARC)

the skin as dusk approaches on this September evening, as they huddle for warmth around a camp-fire. Harriet Jones was there with some of her 15 children and her father, Alfred Price Jones. The guests, sitting on upturned buckets, listened as the singing started, beguiled by Mr Jones' voice: 'Out of the half-light came the sound of a beautiful tenor voice singing,' said Leather,

> It is difficult to convey to those who have never known the joy of hearing folk songs as we heard that ballad; the difference between hearing it there and in a drawing room or concert hall, is just that between discovering a wild flower growing in its native habitat, and admiring it when transplanted to a botanical garden.

Vaughan Williams was equally entranced, writing of a magical evening of musical notes floating in the air, falling down around and captivating him: 'It was a cold, clear September night and we were by the blazing fire in the open ground of the Gypsy encampment; the fire had been especially lighted to enable us to note down tunes and words in the growing darkness.' It was an evening he would never forget.

It is possible that Mary Carbery knew both the Lockes and Leather and Vaughan Williams. This extraordinary woman's first marriage was to the 9th Baron Carbery of Castle Freke, County Cork, Ireland and she spent many years in the early part of the last century travelling across Europe in a horse-drawn (ox-drawn too, according to some accounts) vardo and spoke fluent Romany. Her grandson from her second marriage, Jeremy Sandford, was in the same mould as Leather and Sharpe, recording the lost music of the Gypsy community. He is better known as the writer of the ground-breaking BBC drama, *Cathy Come Home*. Eton-educated, Sandford grew up at Eye Manor, a historic house in Herefordshire and spent most of his life in the Welsh border country. His fascination with the Gypsy community began early, awakened by his grandmother, Mary Carbery. He almost certainly encountered Gypsy hop pickers and the famous Locke fiddlers. In his book, *Songs from the Roadside: 100 years of Gypsy Music*, Sandford said: 'There were in the early years of this century many Gypsy players on the fiddle. The Locke family, also known as the Gentleman Lockes, travelled to the West Midlands with 20 or 30 donkeys in scarlet harness and were renowned for their fiddle playing.'

Dave Warnes of Yarkhill is a gentleman, nature-lover, aging hippy, biblio-phile and folk musician. In his travels over the last five decades, he has also recorded music and song from the oral tradition, neither written down nor notated, from his time working alongside Gypsy families on hop harvests at Dormington, Claston and Pomona in the late 1970s. On one of his many book-lined shelves is a treasure, a wooden box full of cassette tapes; one is labelled simply, *Gypsy singers Dormington 1976*. Dave's prowess on the guitar made him a welcome nightly guest at their sing-alongs:

> The Jones family came from Merthyr Tydfil and lived in a quarry there in the winter. Richard was the father of the family and Marlene was his wife. They were lovely people and hard-working too, not just hops but fruit-picking, apple-picking, potato-picking; they did all the crops. And when they weren't doing that, they would be sitting around the camp-fire making clothes pegs, little items out of wood, bundling up sprigs of heather to sell door-to-door, that sort of thing. They liked me because I could play the guitar. I've always written songs and I wrote several about Gypsies and hop picking, including one using all Gypsy words, like *gavmush* for policeman, *rom* for road. I had a little notebook with me and would write things down that would probably make a line in a song, so I wrote one about Nelson and Bobby, two of the Gypsies, who were engaged. It was called *Working in Bullion*, which is a variety of hops that are very tough, with coarse leaves, and scratches your arms, a really difficult crop to work in. It was a long time ago, but I remember a couple of verses:
>
> Working in Bullion,
> We'll never make a million
> We'll never make it on the wages we get ...
>
> The Ben Rye that runs this gaff,
> He never seems to smile,
> All he seems to do is moaning all the while.
>
> (Sung to the author in an interview)

The Jones family hand-picking at Larport Court Farm, Mordiford, 1962 (© Derek Evans/ HARC)

Patricia Parkinson, 85, brought up nine children in Welsh Newton Common on the border with Monmouthshire and Herefordshire, where she still lives today. It's a lovely rural spot, quiet, away from busy roads. It's a long way from her childhood in war-torn Peckham in London. In 1939 she was evacuated to Devon for six months before her mother brought her back to the capital. But in 1943, with bombs raining down around them in Lewisham, Patricia's father, who was in the fire service, decided to find a place of safety for Patricia, her mother, and her younger sister. They set off for Whitbourne, a place Patricia had never heard of before:

We went by train to Worcester and then got the Midland Red Bus and got off at the Wheatsheaf at the bottom of Stocking Hill and walked up to the village to the place where we were to stay, the village shop. I had a little rucksack and my teddy bear and a gas mask in a box. I thought it was heaven when I first arrived. I loved the countryside so much. We all slept in one bed. The room was facing the road, and, in the morning, there was the sound like clopping and I leapt out of bed, looked through the window and there was a herd of cows walking to the farm next door. I ran down the stairs and followed them into the farm yard. It was the beginning of a wonderful experience because I went there every day and I learnt how to milk the house cow. I felt I was at home, I felt I was where I should be.

The first morning we were there, everything was sparkling, the nettles, the leaves, the petals, it was autumn time. I was left in charge of my little sister. Dad knew we would have a lot of walking to do and he had made a pushchair for her, like a deck chair. We went down the steep hill and along a rough lane leading off. It was all quiet, nobody about. And that's where I found everyone, that's where the hopyard was, everyone was picking hops. I went home and told my Mother what I had seen. We went back, and we had a half a crib with someone else, it had a partition. After that we went every day.

After the war we came back to London and I discovered the Lewisham Library had a gramophone department and you could go in and borrow two or three records at the time. I came away with one and when it started playing, it was Elgar's *Chanson de Matins*, I was immediately transported back to Whitbourne. That piece of music still has the same effect. My time there was heavenly, and it changed my life.

Hop pickers, including a school boy booker, at Ankerdine, August 1944 (© Peter Walker)

George Cox, Vardo Maker

In June 1960, Hereford master wheelwright, George Cox (the last hand-builder of vardoes in Britain) loaded his hand-crafted vardo, ready for its journey by rail to a Gypsy family in Somerset, who had ordered a model on their way through the city after hop picking in the county. Other families with older vardoes used to stop in Usk on the way home after the harvest, at the barrel-making works in the town, to pick up big barrel hoops, which they used for making and repairing their bow-top wagons, before returning to their winter homes at Canton Common in Cardiff.

Top: George Cox (in glasses) and assistant Albert Wood working on the vardo for the Somerset Gypsy family (© Derek Evans, HARC)

Middle: The same vardo being loaded by George (in braces) at Barr's Court Goods Station, Hereford (*Guardian*, 23 June 1960)

Bottom: George (in hat), aged 73, loading a newly refurbished vardo onto a low-loader for its journey by road to the Lincolnshire estate of Sir Geoffrey Harmsworth, to be used there as a summerhouse (*Birmingham Post*, 17 June 1967)

Another musician and faithful recorder of the oral tradition was Michael Raven. In the 1990s, he met a young musician, Peter Delaney, who was camped on Eyton Common near Leominster while working on the hops at Brierley Court. Michael recorded Delaney's words. It is an unromantic and, unusually, a contemporary view of the picking season and the 'beast', the picking machine.

Its hop-pickers wanted on minimum pay,
Come feed the hop-eater ten hours a day,
No qualifications or union card,
It's false names only in Herefordshire Hopyards.

At the crack of dawn, the great beast awakes
With an almighty roar the whole shed it shakes,
It screams, and it rages and roars to be fed,
And the humans out front hang till they feel dead.

Down in the hopyard, come sun or come rain,
The crow's in his nest but he can't fly away;
The tractors keep coming for load after load,
And the bine cutters sharpen their knives on their stones.
Up in the hop shed the beast's belly so full,
It's spewing out hops into sacks by the ton,
Then carry them into the kilns to be dried,
Where the kiln workers sweat till their brains are fried.

As dusk comes in the great beast gives a sigh,
And falls down to sleep fast as any man could die,
The pickers go home, they've no thought for next day,
For tonight they'll be drunk on their minimum pay.

A Guide to Herefordshire, 1996

3

Growing the Hop:
the growers

Those tall bare poles, that elaborately knotted string, those ploughed acres – what does it all mean? The explanation is forthcoming: it is English beer.

Vita Sackville-West, *Country Notes*, 1939

THE hop industry in the West Midlands has lost a number of extraordinary alumni in recent years, including Graham Andrews, Peter Davies, Barry Parker and John Probert to name a few. The next generation of growers continues to embrace new hop varieties, engineering and technology, but there are some elements of hop husbandry that are unchanged: existing roots cut back, new ones planted, hopyards repaired, new ones erected, ground prepared, labour force appointed, hops ploughed up, hops ploughed down, muck spreading, stocking hops, cutting and harrowing hops, picking machine maintained. All this to bring flavour to beer. There is a lot to do and there is a lot at stake. There is no let-up: the cultivation of hops involves work for almost every season of the year.

The hop-growing community is often described as one big family, generations strong in many cases. But not for Geoff Thompson. When he started growing hops at Little Lambswick Farm, Lindridge, near Tenbury Wells (from 1978 to 2018) he was unusual in being new to the industry (although not to farming). In later years, his hops won countless awards, and his skill as a hop grower gained him some hard-won respect from other growers. It was some of the aforementioned elder statesmen who helped and advised him in his early days, sharing their knowledge and expertise of hop farming with this newcomer. Geoff:

My father already had Oldfields Farm, then we had the good fortune to rent the adjacent farm, Little Lambswick. This gave us the opportunity to grow hops for the first time. It was a typical Teme Valley farm with fruit and hops, grassland and cereals. Part of the farm runs along the River Teme which had wonderfully deep, silty soil, perfect for hop growing. But we knew nothing about hops and had so much to learn.

It was quite something for someone out of the industry to take on a hop farm as most farms have been in hop-growing families for generations. Over the years, as we gained experience and confidence we managed to gain respect amongst our fellow growers.

Fortunately, my friend and neighbour, Richard Elliot, was an established grower and helped us immensely in the first few years, and so many others have been there to advise and help over the years too, including John Spilsbury and Graham Andrews, who both took me under their wing and shared their knowledge to help me prosper in my hop-growing career, both exceptional people.

You have to be a certain type of person to be a hop grower, extremely motivated and dedicated to the attention to detail that is needed to grow the crop, which is particularly challenging. Growing hops is definitely addictive, and you have to be slightly mad to consider growing it. It can drive you to total distraction at times. It can also give you incredible rewards.

Pole pullers, Tenbury (© Tom Tolley & Christine Tipton)

I don't have blood in my veins, I have hop juice. **Raymond (Ray) Morris**
Ray Morris, 73, of Burford Mill Farm, Shropshire, is a fifth-generation grower.
His son Thomas has picked up the reins now, but Ray remains involved. It
is hard to retire from hops. Like others from this 'small band of brothers',
the Morrises are looking to the future and have expanded their hop acreage:

> My father moved here in 1935 as a tenant of the Burford Estate, but
> he was growing hops before that. We are the only growers left in
> Shropshire, the most northern grower in the country, and the most
> northerly in the northern hemisphere. Not many of us left now, but I've
> got that determination. It's such a tradition and I'm just one of these
> traditionalists and I've just kept it going. There have been years when
> I've made good money, and years when I've made none. I'm just addicted
> to hops and I won't be beat. When the going gets tough the tough get
> going! You need that to grow hops.

The Walker family of Knightwick represent early pioneers and scions of the
hop-growing fraternity. In the 1930s they motorised a mobile spraying unit,
using an old Model-T engine mounted on a cart. It worked very well. This
forward thinking was some light years away for wagoner Joseph Lewey. He
was still part of the old guard as agriculture transitioned to mechanisation.
He arrived at Leighton Court, Stretton Grandison, in the post-First World
War years and he was a man who took great pride in his role in the hopyard.
At the end of his working life, he recorded in careful writing, with wonderful
illustrations, the right and proper way to work a team of horses in the close
confines of a hopyard: 'They all have names; two were called Farmer, the
others were Duke, Trooper, Shorty, Norman, Dragon and Brittan. As a wagoner, you have to look after them. You need them in the hopyard.'

Joseph Newey was born in 1905, a native of Kings Norton. He completed
his farm apprenticeship at Grange Farm, Alvechurch soon after the First
World War, and in 1921 he became official farm pupil at Leighton Court, a
stock-rearing and hop farm. Cattle feed and charcoal for the kilns arrived
in rail wagons at nearby Stoke Edith Station, from where it was fetched in
horse-drawn carts. In the decades before the tractor became widely used, all
motive power came from horses, and Joseph was very proud of his horses at
Leighton Court:

A good horse could be bought for £70 then. When I was promoted from team driver to ploughman, a Gypsy boy became my driver. The horses had to be shod regularly and for this we went to the blacksmith at Bishops Frome. There were no telephones, so no appointments made. You just turned up and you often had to wait while earlier arrivals were shod first. After the hop picking the Gypsies would bring their horses to be shod and you could have between ten and fifteen waiting for the blacksmith.

On a hop farm a wagoner was a skilled man who had to work hard. Ploughing and hoeing were very specialised jobs, as the rows were very close together, and Shire horses were very big and their work harnesses bulky. We used to plough between the rows so that one furrow fell over the plants, then down the middle to leave a hollow (*see ploughing diagram opposite*). We left it then 'til the spring, when we reversed the process, ploughing the furrows back into the hollow. This left a row of hop roots six- to eight-inches wide, still covered with soil, as a ridge. Then we employed casual labour, usually Gypsies, to knock down the remaining ridge and then cut the revealed hop plant down to soil level. We used to stop now and then for a chat and some cider. Later on, when the flowers formed, you took a machine, which blowed powdered sulphate onto the plants round the yard. That was a horrid job.

Joseph would have had some advice and possibly some stern words for a young Terry Chandler of Ledbury, who had a near-disaster in 1960 at Bransford, doing a similar job but with a tractor. The sight of a collapsed hopyard is one no grower ever wants to see. Neither did Terry:

During the summer the hops were sprayed to kill off the bugs and prevent hop wilt. At the same time the rows between the hop vines were continually hoed with a tractor and harrows to kill off the weeds. I was hoeing one day just after the hops had been sprayed, on my little grey Ferguson, when all of a sudden, bang, crash, and the sound of the hop wires breaking and falling down. I thought the whole yard was falling down, but it was in fact just a few. I had fallen asleep due to the spray and smashed a hop pole down. I was lucky. Thankfully there wasn't much damage done.

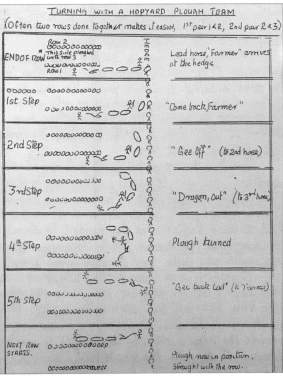

TURNING WITH A HOPYARD PLOUGH TEAM

(Often two rows done together makes it easier, 1st pair 1&2, 2nd pair 2&3)

END OF ROW	Row 2 / This side ploughed with row 3 / Row 1	Lead horse "Farmer" arrives at the hedge
1st Step		"Come back, Farmer"
2nd Step		"Gee off" (to 2nd horse)
3rd Step		"Dragon, out" (to 3rd horse)
4th Step		Plough turned
5th Step		"Get back Lad" (to Farmer)
NEXT ROW STARTS.		Plough now in position, straight with the row.

Clockwise from top: Ploughing among the hop poles (© Miss White); Ray Whiting of Pridewood Hops in a hopyard with horse and wagon (© P. Andrews); A wagoner at Carwardine (© John Griffiths); Hopyard ploughing diagram by Joseph Newey (© HARC)

Two halves of two stereoscopic photographs made by Alfred Watkins in the early twentieth century, showing a hopyard early in the growing season (*left*) and with hops maturing (*right*). The left-hand image shows both the older method of growing hops up poles, and the later method of training hops up a trellis of strings and wirework (© Hereford Libraries)

THE HOP POLE – POLING

Wirework – a high trellis of wire and string supporting the growing crop – became the dominant method for growing hops through the twentieth century and into the twenty-first, replacing the previous method of using simple poles. Separate poles were thrust into the ground next to each root, and, as the hop grew, it wound its way up and around the poles, rather as ivy grows around a telegraph pole. Each pole only lasted a few years, so many thousands were grown in coppice plantations, a significant and profitable side-industry to hop growing. The widespread adoption of wirework in the hopyard from the beginning of the twentieth century made redundant this age-old practice, changing the profile of the landscape that had hitherto displayed singular, erect, spindly columns, wavering lightly in the winds, hop bines clinging on as their tendrils reached to the sky.

Hop poles were valuable to the grower and their theft was taken seriously. Walter Hill, a hawker picking hops with his family at Lindridge, was caught stealing a quantity of them, total value 1/-, from Woodston farm in 1907. Unfortunately for him, PC Jones was in the vicinity and Hill was caught red-handed. PC Jones told the court: 'He was carrying the hop poles which were produced from under his arm!' Poor old Hill. He pleaded guilty but explained all he wanted was some wood 'to make a fire to have some tea for my children.' The court was sympathetic, but an example had to be made, and he was fined 5/-, an enormous sum for a man already on his uppers.

GEORGE HOPKINS, 90, LEDBURY

I was born in a hop field, sort of! We lived in a cottage surrounded by them at Whittick Manor, Newtown. My life has been in hops. George Hopkins
George Hopkins has lived and breathed hops all his working life. Before him his father worked with them too, as a hop-dryer at Bosbury. On 1 January 1944 at the age of 14, George started his life-long career at the Town Farm, Castle Frome:

> One of the changing scenes of the countryside was every farmer who grew hops needed poles and you'd find them somewhere on that farm, usually a couple of acres of coppicing, most often ash. And when they were about 15-foot tall or so, they used to cut them off, so they had some fresh poles every year. They'd only last for three or four years because they eventually broke off at ground level and you might use them for another year, but eventually they got too short. That's how they survived then. They planned ahead a bit and grew the poles.

Ray Morris's father grew hops on poles too:

> Wirework had yet to reach these parts. Poles were equivalent to bean sticks. A statute acre is a thousand roots, so you imagine two sticks to a root, and you had to put them all in with an iron bar and then tie them at the top with raffia. So that's 3,000 poles. Imagine the amount of labour when they were going in every spring. They were coppiced, these poles. Every eight years the withy beds, and the ash beds, they were grown up just the right size and then they used to coppice them.

Overleaf: Preparing hop poles, 1934 (© Herefordshire Histories)

Hop poles being carted through Ledbury (© Chris Ponter)

Edwardian hop pickers, picking pole-grown hops into a crib (© Neil Wright)

Monica Symonds, 87, of Bishops Frome is a member of a legion of forgotten, uncomplaining, hard-working women who worked the land to feed children and put food on the table and fuel in the fire. Even as a child she kept busy, accompanying her dad. She's only slowed down in recent years, reluctantly:

> I picked hops with Dad years ago at Wellington near Bromyard, hops up a pole. You had to cut them off the pole first, then roll them off, and then unwind them. Once you hacked the hop off you took the pole out and leant it over the crib and cut them off. Poles used to be thrown down and then used for the next year. My dad used to put them in ready for the hops to go back up.

Several decades before Monica, Ellen Partridge (neé Clews) was born into a Suckley farming family in 1904. Her parents, Frederick and Ann, kept cattle, sheep, hops and Shire horses at Yearsett Court in the village. Baking bread and making butter to sell in Worcester, travelling from Suckley Station, was routine for this young woman. Other times she would take her pony and trap. In her delightful account of life on the farm, she described the pole pitchers of her youth:

> We used to have two men pitch the hop poles. They were called the pole pitchers and they had as much cider as they wanted. We used the same poles twice and we used to take the broken pieces home for firewood. One man was called Snatchfold and the other Parton. He went to the First World War and the day it finished, he was kicked by a mule and died!
>
> During that war it was difficult to get labour with the men away and the women working at the ammunition factory in Hereford, so Father got exemption for my brother, sister and me to have time off school to tie the hops. There was no wirework in those days, just poles. And because of the war, we couldn't get raffia, which was used to tie the hops to the poles with, so we had to use bulrushes, and just as you thought you had tied it well, they broke, and you had to start again. I hated it. I was always last going up to dinner and last coming back.

After the harvest, the poles were stacked in wigwam-like formations, ready for the next year. In the first decade of the twentieth century, when airborne flight was in its infancy, an aeroplane flew over Burton Farm hop grounds, frightening a group of women working in the fields, who fled to the shelter of one of these wigwams until the offender disappeared. 'They had never seen a plane before,' said Ray Morris.

Stacks of hop poles in a Ledbury hopyard, c.1930 (*top*, Alfred Watkins © Hereford Libraries) and at Stoke Edith in the early twentieth century (*bottom*, © Zimmerman archive)

By 1931, Hereford author and photographer Alfred Watkins was bemoaning the decline in the use of traditional hop poles, while chronicling the spread of a new type of hopyard:

> The multitude of poles formerly used in our hopyards is a disappearing
> feature which greatly added to the picturesqueness of the countryside
> in this, the second largest hop-acreage county in England. Twelve to
> fifteen feet high, they were all grown in local coppices, and each season
> were newly 'pitched' close together in the hop-rows, being the only
> support for the hop-bines to climb. A bare forest of sticks until the tender
> tendrils crept from the ground in spring to climb them. Then greener
> and greener, until in full flower. Then came the busy picking season, a
> more picturesque scene than the harvest in vineyards. The bines were
> cut at the base, and the poles pulled and laid over the picking cribs.
> During the winter the hopyards were dotted with wigwam-like stacks
> of the poles at regular intervals striding the ploughed furrows between
> the rows of plants, now hidden in the ground. The wire work which has
> almost superseded all this consists of far fewer but heavier poles in wider
> intervals like telephone poles, with cross-bar at top and two strands of
> horizontal wire, there being one line of wire at the foot. The hops do
> not climb the wire, but up perpendicular strings threaded up and down
> between the wires. Poles and wires remain on the ground all the year
> round, a rather ugly prediction for next September's crop. And the poles,
> alas, seldom come from native coppices, but are imported.
>
> *The Masefield Country*, 1931

Wood preservatives, such as creosote, arrived on the scene from the early 1860s. It caused a quiet revolution in farming. The legacy of that can still be seen today according to Ray Morris: 'They used to use the old hop poles for hedging you see, and you still come across the odd one. Even now if you go to lay an old hedge, you'll find a post that has gone past and broken off, and the bottom half is so well creosoted.'

Wood preservative also marked the arrival of noxious pickling tanks on hop farms, vessels long enough to accommodate poles, with a fire crackling underneath. Pickling poles was a dirty, smelly and hazardous job. George Hopkins: 'All the big farms had their own tar tank. It would probably be about the size of an average living room and had a furnace underneath and you would keep shovelling coal under to keep boiling the tar. It was a horrible and dangerous job.' Once the correct temperature was reached, poles were dipped, submerged and pickled. There were other pickling tanks at the bottom of Long Meadow, close to Childer Wood, Castle Frome, and at the Trumpet Inn, a syndicate of growers pressure-creosoted their poles, doing away with more old-fashioned methods.

During the Second World War, a 17-year-old German prisoner-of-war, Reinhold, got up to some mischief. He and his fellow POW, Mueller, cycled from Tenbury up to Bank Farm, Rochford, to help on the Powell farm, preparing hop poles. David Powell:

> Dad used to have them in the green and the Germans used to take all the peel off them and then we had to creosote them down at Newnham Farms because we didn't have a creosote tank long enough to take them. They were about 20-feet long, a big tank with a fire underneath with a chimney and a damper. I don't know why, but Reinhold, who became a great friend of mine, pulled the damper out and threw it away! The fire started to roar and the creosote started to bubble right to the top. We couldn't find the damper for quite a while but they finally found it in a lot of timber. He was like the devil!

Pity the agonies of 34-year-old farm labourer Edward Smith who died in April 1930 after falling into a vat of boiling creosote. Smith was working at the Pard House Farm, Shelsley Kings. He was accustomed to creosoting hop poles, said the inquest, it was all part of his job. A fire was alight beneath the tank and the contents were simmering at the time of the accident. After unloading the poles from the tank, Mr Smith placed a plank across in order to reach the remaining poles more easily. The plank gave way and he fell in, suffering horrific burns. The Coroner recorded a verdict of accidental death.

Early in 1900 the spectre of a new hop-growing system began to cause concern for owners of hop-pole plantations. There was a plea, careers advice even, in the *Evesham Chronicle* in September of that year:

> For a very long period, hop-pole culture has been the mainstay of owners of plantations, and the number of poles, from 14ft to 20ft long and as

thick as one's arm, has been enormous. But there is no doubt hop-pole growing is becoming a thing of the past and it would be rendering a service to owners like myself, who will now have to grow timber instead of poles, if someone could suggest the best method of making the change, bearing in mind, that hop coppice as it stands is very much mixed.

Wood preservatives was a leap forward for hop growers; the introduction of wirework was another.

WIREWORK — BUILDING THE FRAMEWORK

Building a hopyard is a serious undertaking and commitment for the hop grower. It costs a lot of money and requires huge amounts of skill and know-how. Wirework carries the hop crop as it grows and the mathematical precision required to erect it involves craftsmanship and techniques often passed down the family line.

The innovator of the wirework growing method in 1863 was Tom Butcher of Selling in Kent. His design reduced the number of poles used by the old method by more than half. Three years later, E.G. Bomford of Evesham and Edwin Farmer of Kyrewood, Tenbury, developed a system using vertical strings tied to two ground-level horizontal wires and two overhead wires joined to posts 15 to 20-feet apart. This system gained in popularity in the West Midlands hop-growing districts and remains little changed today.

Freshly-strung wirework at Guinness Brewery hopyards, Braces Leigh Farm (© Charlie Morris)

Erection of new hopyard and repairs to existing yard

Hop Marketing Board costings notebook, 1958
Messrs Gallimore and Parry, Priors Court, Staplow, Ledbury

Week ending November 1st – wages raised.

32 anchor blocks

32 anchor rods

11 eye bolts

11 plates

25 inside poles

15 anchor poles

17 coils '00' wire – 17 cwts

Wirework repairs week ending November 8th:

W. Wacker – dig anchors & fix blocks – 32½ hours

A. Hughes – dig anchor holes & fill in – 36 hours

R. Mitchell – haul wirework materials – 2 hours (David Brown & trailer)

Week ending December 6th:

T. Jones & R. Allen – hauling hop poles & collecting old posts – 7 x 2 hours

W. Wacker – digging anchor holes & wire straining 'pump' – 25½ hours

S. Trigg – hedge trim around hopyards – 13 hours

A collapsed hopyard is prohibitively costly for the grower, and can potentially amount to many thousands of pounds to repair. But it has happened. In September 1950 *The Ross Gazette* reported on a storm that wreaked chaos for one grower: 'Gales brought havoc when picking was about to commence. At a Yarkhill farm 16½ acres were blown down through wire snaps and, in this instance, the hops were the best of an exceptionally good crop.'

A hop crop in full leaf is very heavy, and for this reason the wirework has to be anchored well enough to be able to withstand all weather conditions.

Man-made windbreaks, tall hedges or lines of poplar trees have all provided shelter in the past. There are other factors to consider too when planning a new hopyard: the lie of the land, the direction of the sun, even the variety of hop.

A great deal rests on getting the framework right, holding, carrying and supporting many tons of plant material under all weather conditions. The wireworker's lot is practical, pragmatic, agricultural work, but there is more to it than that. There are mathematical complexities, but also artfulness in the straight, taut lines following the earth's contours. As the number of hopyards decline, so too do the experts in their construction. Bert Barnett was one. His son John grew up in the thick of hop-growing country at Stretton Grandison and followed his father into hops in the 1950s:

> He must have built hundreds of them. And by building, I mean he did all the wirework. He used ladders to do it but didn't wear hard hats or anything. Didn't have those things in them days. It was a full-time job in the winter. He showed those coming up behind him how to do it. There was a real skill, people don't realise that.

When hop growing returned to Bank Farm, Rochford in the 1946–47 season, it was Bert who was engaged by the Powell family to erect their 10 acres of wirework. He had some help though, said David Powell, who took over from his father, but ceased growing in 1998: 'We had our own staff helping him, plus some German prisoners-of-war. They dug most of the anchor holes by hand, and dad bought most of the hop cuttings from existing growers.'

Another man whose expertise was called upon across the hop-growing district was Norman Watkins of Bishops Frome. He learnt the trade from his father, Ned. Norman's large family often helped. His daughter Sue remembers a hard-working man:

> He was not an academic, but he knew everything there was to know in the hop world. He was so respected. His life was completely in hops, working for Paskes of Lyde for years. All the anchor wires, all the tensioning, it was all done by hand. Because the repairs to hopyards were usually done in the winter, he worked in some awful conditions. As a family, we used to go to help and do the setting out with him, often in freezing cold weather,

with an armful of pegs passing them to my brother who would put it in the ground on his marker line. Mum kept us warm by making tea and putting it in thick Bulmer flagons wrapped in big woolly socks.

One of Norman's regular customers were the Hancocks of Wyercroft, Bishops Frome. Rob Hancocks would consider no one else at one time:

When I left school in the 1980s, there were still a lot of these old boys on the farm that had that hop knowledge. None of it was written down. They just had it, learnt it somehow. Norman Watkins was one of them. He did all the wire-working round here. A lot of these old boys worked for him and they all used to go off wire-working in a van with him. Didn't matter what the weather was like. There's no doubt Norman Watkins dominated the wire-working round here.

Attaching hooks to the wirework on Bank Farm, Rochford (© David Powell)

With a dwindling demand for hops, the hopyard wirework is taken down at Bank Farm, Rochford in 2003 (© David Powell)

Mervyn Carless is this country's last contract wireworker. He learned his skills from his father Peter, one of Bert's early pupils. In his 50s, he has built hopyards for the likes of Formula 1's Jody Schechter and Paul McCartney (who created an ale using hops grown on his land in East Sussex, called 'Old Stinkhorn' after the distinctive fungi that grow on his estate there). Mervyn:

I always say I was born in a hop crib. My father worked for Bert Barnett in the Ledbury area and when he finished, he left the goodwill and customers to Dad. So, I learnt the business from him. Things really haven't changed since Bert, but Dad did find ways of improvising and making things better and easier. We lived in the hamlet of Lower Eggleton and there were quite a lot of small farms that had an average of around 20/30 acres of hops and they all needed some work doing repair-wise and that's how I started, and I haven't really stopped. When Dad started, he was living in Newtown. At that time there were so many hops you could walk through hopyards all the way from Hereford to Worcester.

Even now when I look at a finished yard, I do feel a sense of pride. You look back at the structure and think, "I did a good job there". It's a lot more technical than people think. We're sometimes treated as agricultural labour but putting up a hopyard is like putting up a building, and even more so with the wind factor involved. People look at it and say, "oh, it's just a hopyard", but there's a colossal weight when the wind blows. It's like a sail on a ship; say you've got 800 hop bines to the acre, and you've got eight acres, and the wind blows, and then you've got the added weight

Peter and Mervyn Carless, hop wireworkers; erecting a new hopyard (© Mervyn Carless)

Norman Watkins and Frank Price erecting a hopyard at Upper Lyde in 1962/ '63
(© Paskes/ Hop Pocket Hop Museum)

of rain; it's got to withstand all that. I've seen some disasters in my time, but not in my yards. I'm quite proud of what I've achieved over the years, because my yards have stood the test of time. I put one up at Burford Mill, over 30 years ago and it's still going strong, and I did another for Philip Clift in the Teme Valley that was 22 feet! That's pretty high.

Philip Price, 80, of Withington was farm manager for the Hawkins family at Thinghill Court. While not a wireworker per se, he was from a particular mould of farm workers and farm foremen worth their weight in gold – hard-working, uncomplaining, proud, getting the job done with the minimum of fuss, and with humour:

I did build one hopyard from scratch once, about ten or twelve acres, at Rushall below the Hall Court. Had a couple of students with me, we put the anchors in, dug the big holes, put anchor rods down, nut on the bottom to hold the block up, and when you strung the wires you pulled the whole lot up tight. It is a lot more complex than it looks. We didn't do a lot of working out in those days. They said "that's where I want it", and that's what we did!

WIREWORKERS — ON STILTS

The first-ever International Stiltwalkers Festival will be held in Merchtem, Belgium next year, with groups from France, Holland, Belgium and England. English stiltwalkers who would like to compete are invited to contact Mr Jean-Paul Van der Elst, Merchtem, Belgium. The journal of the Hop Marketing Board, November 1982

The tractor and crow's nest, or even a ladder, seem an obvious choice when it comes to the construction of intricate wirework. But not for everyone. Some believed there was a far more practical way of doing this: on stilts.

Geoff Godsell of Bishops Frome died in 2019 aged 94. Still handsome in his later years, as a young man he bore a close resemblance to Clint Eastwood. But would that Hollywood hard man work an eight-hour day on wirework 16 feet up, on stilts? Geoff did, and other stilt-walkers like him did too.

Geoff grew up on a smallholding in Felton, near to Ullingswick and could have followed his father and become a carpenter and wheelwright. But instead,

Geoff Godsell on stilts (© Kevin Godsell)

at 17 and in the midst of the Second World War, he tried to join the RAF. Rejected because of his age, he tried the Merchant Navy instead, and was soon part of the Atlantic Convoys. In 1945 his boat left New York and on the journey across the Atlantic it was torpedoed, leaving him seriously injured and many of his crewmates dead. He was taken to Newfoundland and eventually returned home after a long recuperation, back to country life, hops and married life in Bishops Frome, with his beloved wife, Peggy.

Geoff's son Kevin lives in Bromyard. His father's photographs are pinned up on the living room walls. As a young man, Kevin followed his father into the industry, but not on stilts:

Dad built a lot of hopyards from scratch. His very first, about 18 feet high, was still standing at Tarrington in 2020 and hops are still growing on it now. He was proud of that. He always used stilts. A hopyard had cross-wires, the carrying wires or load-bearing wires, and then no.6 wires that went the length of the yard: these are what the hops used to hang on, the small wires that were tied off. These had to be tied together with smaller pieces of wire. To do this Dad would use stilts. He had another man working with him, John Taylor, also of Bishops Frome. He worked for Dad for a long time, the best worker he had. Not many men are keen on getting up on stilts. I wasn't.

Dad's stilts were sort of like scaffolding pipes, hollow metal tubes, but heavy, very heavy. He would have straps over his feet then around his knees and then his waist and at the bottom of the tubes were fixed two blocks of wood to help him balance. To get up on them he climbed a ladder leaning against a pole. They were actually quite stable. John Taylor used to have a radio strapped to his back and sandwiches in a bag when he was working so he didn't have to go back down again. They'd be up there all day.

Geoff's patch included Townend Hop Farm at Bosbury, Frogend at Bishops Frome, Lady Wacktor of Suckley, and Claston and Dormington Court for Peter Davies. Peter enjoyed a strong friendship with Geoff and in the early 1980s, when Allied Breweries (Davies was Director of Dormington Court Hop Farms Ltd DCHF, a subsidiary of Allied Breweries UK Ltd) extended their hop-growing enterprise with the purchase of Brierley Court near Leominster, he contracted Geoff to build 250 statute acres of hopyards. It was a mammoth exercise.

His prowess at measuring out new hopyards had other uses too, particularly in the sports fields of Bishops Frome. Rob Hancocks: 'Geoff used to mark out all the hopyards so he was the obvious choice to mark out our football pitch here because he knew how to mark everything out accurately. He was the only man for that job.'

In the twenty-first century, Leominster's hop growers are few in number. But it was not always so. Stone carvings of hops on corbels at the Catholic church hint at its prominence here once upon a time. Brierley Court Farm could not have gone unnoticed. It was an operation of near epic proportions: a 250-acre hop farm built from scratch. It was estimated that by the time the yards were ready to grow hops, 16,666 poles had been set up, secured with 3,750 anchor blocks, supporting 150 tons of wire. James Sufton, Davies' neighbour and fellow hop grower at Larport, watched the yards grow at Davies' invitation, and was impressed with the sheer scale and ambition of the enterprise. DCHF's immodest promotional literature at the time claimed that this 'new hop farm will produce hops worth £1 million'. But one rueful grower observed that, 'you would want to make that much to cover the cost of putting the bloody yard up in the first place'. Within ten years, Allied Breweries had moved on, after a kiln fire. There are no hopyards there now. Geoff, with Kevin working for him, was on the site for three years. Kevin:

> His original contract was to put up 250 statute acres in five years, but he did it in three. I was there with another three or four guys. He sometimes looked for more workers through the Job Centre, but they would turn up at the gate, take one look at what we were doing, and walk away! Never saw them again.

This was not a job for fair-weather types. It was tough and physical, and winter time was particularly harsh. Geoff ignored strong winds, plummeting temperatures which froze his hands to the poles and cuts and bruises from snapped wires. In his sixties, after the premature death of his wife, he retired from stilt-walking and turned to tutoring at Hereford Technical College in the 1980s on their first ever hop-growing course. Philip Price is another from the small band of stilt-walkers (all men, no women found as yet), this time at Thinghill Court for the Hawkins family. Philip was not fazed easily, just another day's work at the farm. But not for his father:

> Dad never did stilts. I think it was only the fools that went up on them. I suppose we were young and stupid. We had our own carpenter on the estate and he used to make the stilts. They were wooden with a little platform where your feet went. There were always spare wellies hanging

around a farm and a pair of these were nailed onto the platform. You took your shoes off and, when you got up there, you put your feet in these wellies, and then just hang on the wires and walk along the yard strapping the little wires to the main ones. But if we left our boots on the ground, when we came down for breakfast or dinner, they would have been filled with water by the other men for a joke! So, then we used to hang them up on the wires, so they couldn't get to them.

It was while working on stilts that Philip inadvertently became involved in a police hunt:

We had some Welsh people living on the farm and the police came to find one man; he obviously was in trouble. I was working up on the stilts with another man, a Welshman, and the police were down in the hopyard with police dogs, shouting someone's name. And they shouted up to me, "where is he?" And I said, "well he ain't going anywhere". "Why?" Well, he's over there, up on them stilts!"

Whether by tractor or stilts, the first part of the hopyard is prepared, anchor blocks buried, wires tightened and taut, hooks in place and secured above, pegs driven into the ground, peeping above the soil, in place by the root. Now it is the turn for the next wave, the stringers.

STRINGING — 'IT'S A BIT LIKE KNITTING'
This activity is still carried out by hand each year. The string (coir) held in a pouch, is strung up onto the top hooks of the wirework and down to the ground pegs, using a long pole called a monkey, with a hollow tube at one end. When complete, the pair of strings from each root are braced together at waist height using binder twine. The Harp, Guinness Staff Magazine, 1973
Come March into April, hopyards across the West Midlands are dotted with moving figures, a choreographed dance to the music of coir rushing through metal, up, down, across, up again, covering the landscape with a crochet-like canopy. Technological advances have not changed this labour-intensive practise. For many, it is less a chore, more a joy.

Cap on (or headscarf — women strung too), hessian bag to the side, they stoop and stretch all day, covering acres. The stringer adds the next layer of

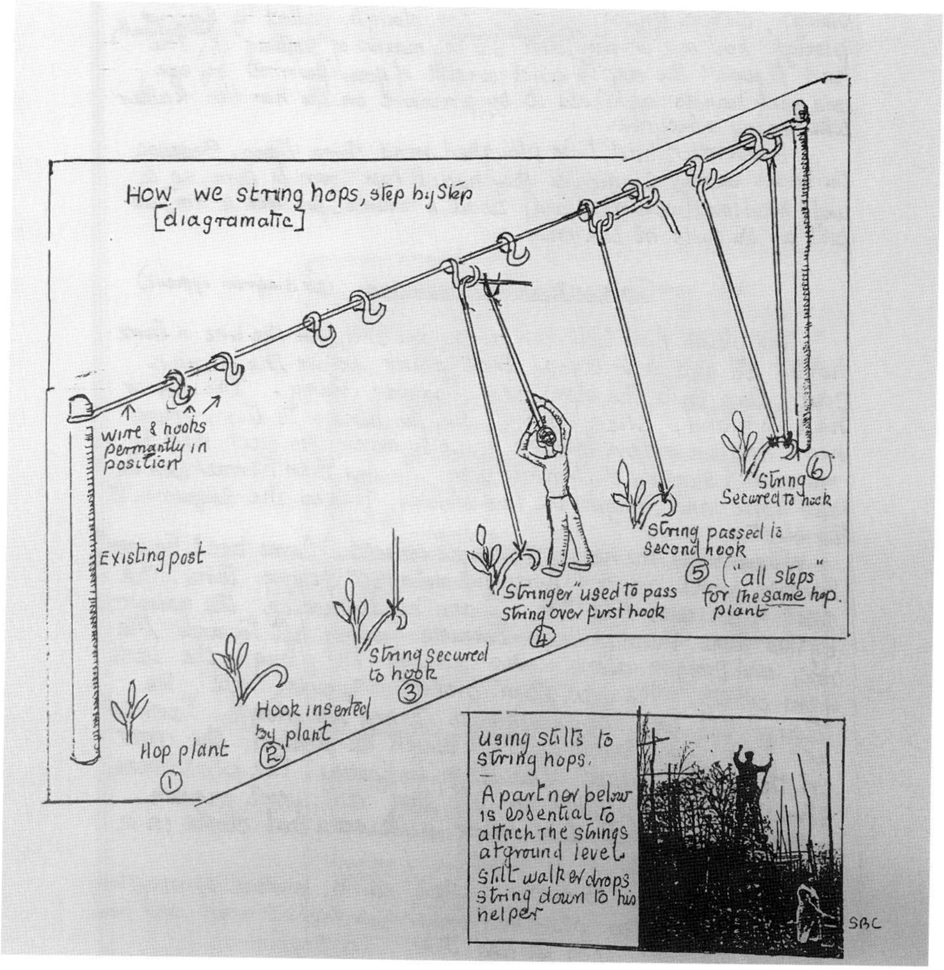
How we string hops, step by step
[diagramatic]
wire & hooks permantly in position
Existing post
Hop plant
1
Hook inserted by plant
2
String secured to hook
3
"Stringer" used to pass string over first hook
4
String passed to second hook
5
("all steps" for the same hop plant
String secured to hook
6
Using stilts to string hops.
A partner below is essential to attach the strings at ground level. Stilt walker drops string down to his helper
SBC

Joseph Newey's illustration of how to string a hopyard (© HARC)

the canopy, an agricultural job that is artisanal in nature, rhythmic, measured, steady, precise, effective, the coir unspooling as it passes through the eye of the 'needle', the monkey. The rough texture of the coir gives hop tendrils something to firmly cling to as they reach up. The stringer uses a long tool, the monkey, the threading part. Already in place close to the hop roots are metal pegs; above hang hooks from the wirework. As the stringers work, they loop the coir around the hook at the top on the cross wire and then back down to the root and the peg, making a vertical zig-zag pattern across the hopyard. In partnership with the wirework, the stringing completes the

Stringing a hopyard using a horse-drawn platform (© Miss White)

mesh-like canopy on which the hops will twist themselves skyward following the sun, cones drooping heavily, like cake mix from a wooden spoon. The stringer's skill is to leave a hopyard that is strong, robust and will stand the test of time: the growing season. At the end of the day, the scene is uniform, beautiful, bristling lightly in the breeze.

Ray Morris compares the process to knitting:

> It's quite an intricate job, a skilled one. I like stringing but a lot of people when they've had about ten minutes say they've had enough! The stringer has to put them on such an angle. I liken it to knitting. Once he gets used to it and get in the flow, get a rhythm, I could do about an acre and a half a day. I knew someone who used to do two or three acres a day on piece work, but it wouldn't be so tidy, and we do it tidy.

In 1973 the Guinness staff magazine carried a photograph of the winners of a hop-stringing and banding-in competition in Kent captioned 'the only event of its kind in the world'. That would have surprised veteran champion stringer George Hopkins and his wife, Lil, a champion bracer. George still has his tankard from a 1958 stringing win at Millend, Castle Frome, and Lil (they always worked in pairs) lost her trophy although she grabbed first prize for bracing. George is not sure how many acres he has strung over the course of his working life, but it probably runs into many thousands. He is sure of one thing though; he enjoyed every single inch of them, every peg, every hook, every loop:

I taught myself to string, but I probably watched a fair few do it before. When you're doing the stringing, you don't want it going straight up, you want an angle. To do it you used to have a nut-stick or something very light, and you had a bit of metal on the end of it and you threaded the string through it. I used to make my own.

I used to do a bit more than most, three-acres or 3,000 roots a day. If it was going well, I've managed to do four and that was about ten or twelve hours a day. I'll tell you, that bag of string got heavier as the day went on. But I took pride in it, oh yes, you had to because how good a job you made of the stringing set the rest of the season. It's got to be tight enough not to be a nuisance to anything else. On the other hand, if it's too tight then it's in danger of snapping off. Oh, but I enjoyed it.

George Hopkins stringing a hopyard at Millend (© George and Lil Hopkins)

Above: Stringing an old-style hop-pole yard (© Miss White)
Opposite: Stringing a wirework hopyard using a 'monkey' (© Miss White)

Philip Price also made his own monkey:

> Oh yes, you had your own monkey. Dad's was still stood in the shed when we cleared the house out after he died. You got used to your monkey. It's like your car, you get used to driving that car, you know how it worked and you kept to it. It was just a long pole sanded down to fit your hand. You didn't want anything too thick, but you wanted to be able to grip it well. The string used to run up through your fingers so that used to get a bit sore. You could wear gloves I suppose but we didn't wear gloves very often. They were too expensive.

While not stringing, Monica Symonds used to assist Ned Watkins by doing the pegging:

> Ned used to say to me, "Monica, come with me, we're putting up some new wirework, you have to do the pegging". And so I would go along with the metal pegs, sticking them one way in the ground, and then the other, so the men could do the string work.

Left: Ray Whiting, with 'monkey', stringing at Pridewood Hops, Ashperton (© Pauline Andrews)
Right: Balls of coir at Millend, Castle Frome, ready for stringing (© Lil and George Hopkins)

John Griffiths, 82, of Madley quickly learned that doing stringing on piece-work had its benefits. He ran a successful construction company until his retirement, but his urge to work for himself started over half a century before in a hopyard. Tyberton born, he was already helping at Carwardine hop farm, Lulham, when he was a 15-year-old. In his shed, John still keeps relics from those days: a ball of coir, wire hooks and a kerf (a hoe for moulding hops):

> My uncle worked there and when he retired I more or less took over.
> I learnt to string when I was about 15. There were three or four older
> employees who had been there for years, and I picked the stringing up
> quite quick just by watching them. You had a sack bag with the coiled
> string in it. You could string quite a few rows in a day and when I was
> 17 I decided to go self-employed because I worked out if you worked say
> from 7.30am to 5pm for the farm as an employee, that was it for the day.
> But self-employed I could go on in the evenings and earn a lot more
> money. But it was hard work, you had to be strong. That's why I took it
> for a price.

Piece-work incentivised Philip Price too – he was down from his stilts now and busy stringing:

> I loved my stringing. I did it piece-work, working all hours of the day.
> You strung so many acres and you knew what you had earned. I was
> about 17 when I first did it and I suppose I learnt from Dad. He was a
> good stringer. He showed you what to do and you had to get on with it.
> I could earn good money at stringing. In them days there wasn't much
> money about. It was a long day and you would carry on 'til dark if you
> were on piece-work. You'd have your dinner and take your sandwiches
> and a flask with you. After stringing a hopyard, I would look back and
> think, "yeah, that's a good job".

Ian Heathcote, aged 80, originally from the West Midlands, now lives in Ross-on-Wye. He did an engineering apprenticeship before moving into dairy farming as a young man. When he contracted brucellosis (a bacterial infection) he decided on a change of career – this time into fruit and hops at Stocks Farm, Suckley.

In around 1971 I saw an advertisement in the *Hereford Times* for a general farm worker for fruit and hops with Mark Capper at Stocks Farm. I knew a little bit about fruit but very little about hops. They were alien to me apart from being very nice in beer. In the early days I had to learn everything, planting the hops, putting the pegs in the ground, doing the wirework, stringing, cooking the hops, throwing the hops down, drying the hops, the lot.

I used to check the hopyards, making sure the ground pegs hadn't come out, and walk up and down checking for missing hooks on the wirework above. If there was a hook missing, you'd have to replace it with a hooking pole, which was a long pole with a little adaptor on the end. You would pull a lever and that would crimp it. When Mr Capper wanted a new yard, he would plan it and we would put the lot in. I was working with three old boys, who had been working there since they were in nappies, Ted, Bunn Morris and Bill Friend. Ted and Bunn had been working for Capper all their lives. When the stringing came, we did it as piece-work as an incentive to give us a bit extra. I worked with Bill Friend. We would split the hopyard up and I would say, "I'm going to do the first ten rows" and he would start on the eleventh and do his ten. That way you covered the whole yard and quite a bit of ground too. You got a bit of a rhythm going using a monkey. The hardest bit was feeding nuts to the monkey! When we finished at the end of a day I used to look back and think, "I did that". It was a sense of real pride.

Planting Fuggle roots (8,000 in a day) at Bank Farm, Rochford, June 1998 (© David Powell)

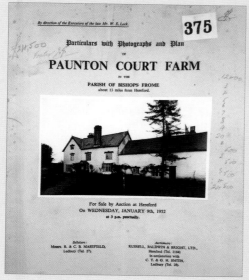

Paunton Court Farm particulars (© Neil Wright)

In January 1952, at the Law Society's rooms in East Street, Hereford, Russell, Baldwin & Bright were under instructions to auction Paunton Court – 'Hop and Mixed Farm' – near Bromyard. It comprised, said the particulars, 'a good house, necessary farm buildings, and modern hop-drying facilities.' No longer growing hops, the magnificently-situated Paunton Court was then, all 169 acres of it, the epitome of hop growing and the riches it could bring. The farm was noted for the quality of its hops (37.5 acres of them), a large proportion being purchased by Bass & Co. Among the particulars noted was:

> The Hop Wirework, 4 Shew Heaters, the 4 Automatic Stokers (Hop Stoker Ltd, Stoke Edith), the Lifter Hairs, Bruff mechanical Hop Bagger, Hand Bagger, Lister 18 h.p. Diesel engine (new 1951), which generates electricity for automatic stokers and works the fans, the Shafting Pulleys, belts and fans, creosote tank with stack and fireplace, all other Hop appliances, Hop fuel and stores.

There was a team of women on the farm done the bracing. So you'd have a stringer in every yard and as I strung my yard they followed you round. **Philip Price**

As the stringers leave the hopyards, there is another army of workers marching in, but in a different uniform. Gone are the cloth caps, jackets, boiler suits, and trousers. In their place are the aprons, pinnies, nylon overalls, cotton dresses, woollen overcoats, headscarves, often with a pram in tow. The army of bracers and trainers has arrived, and they have a lot to squeeze in before school is out.

Janet Parker of Stoke Lacy was born into a hop family, married into a hop family, and her daughter has also married into a hop family. Tying and bracing is second-nature to her:

> All roots had two strings attached. After stringing came the bracing, when the two strings which held the hops were tied together about waist high with a piece of string. After bracing came tying and hops grow very fast, sometimes as much as four to six inches in a single night, so by April or early May they are ready to be tied. Tying is training three hops up each string. Hops will only go one way up a string and that is clockwise. Next came leafing when all the leaves below the bracing strings were stripped off. My sister Mary and I always helped, and you definitely needed gloves for that job as hops are very rough and they can scratch you.

Irene Whiting
bracing hop strings,
Pridewood Hops
(© Pauline Andrews)

Hop tying at Humphrey Nott's hopyard at Kyrewood, Tenbury, 1950s (© Eric Lowe)

Bracers often worked close behind the stringer, pieces of twine at the ready, drawing the three – or four – strings together into the 'bracing line', helping achieve the optimum growing angle. The tying gang, which came after, was busy throughout April and May, training young hop shoots around the strings in a clockwise direction, as the shoots grew, using a twiggling stick, to coax them in the right direction.

Often hidden and silent in the great story of the hop, these women were hard-working, doughty, indomitable and uncomplaining – for the most part. They were out in all weathers, on their hands and knees, sometimes with babes in prams beside them, all to bring much-needed cash into the family purse, moving from one harvest to the next. In their later years, they look back and wonder how they did it, how they kept kith, kin and hearth together. The refrain, 'hard work doesn't kill you', is heard from these women. A ganger assembled a list of workers, and pick-up, in the back of a truck or Land Rover, was arranged at the end of the road and drop-off at the end of the day.

Sheila Payne, 82, lives in a gated community of almshouses today, bright and spacious. At 16 she worked in the laundry at a psychiatric hospital – 'I had a whistle around my neck that I used if I needed help'. When children arrived, working the land was, while hard work, a blessing too. It brought money into the house when there was none, and food on the table when often there was little. And she could bring her children to work with her. Sheila:

> I've had a hard life. Especially when you had a husband who said I'll see you in a few days and didn't know when he was going to come back! He didn't contribute a lot to the household. I didn't even have the rent money and had to ask a neighbour to pay it for me. So, I used to work the land and then go and pay her for the rent. Me and my neighbour, she used to buy the sausages and I used to buy the potatoes and we shared the food. That's how we lived.
>
> At Claston we had to tie all the hops. Jessie was Peter Davies' sister and she used to let us come down in the barn with the kids if it rained. She was really good to us and would take us home at the end of the day. They used to fetch us in a Land Rover and my kids sat on my lap or on the floor. I would make the sandwiches the night before, and pack crisps and a flask. If it was cold, we used to make a fire. It was hard, but I enjoyed it. The tying, going around the one way, and the training, on your knees first then, as they get a bit bigger, you stand and put them round a bit higher. We did that for about two months. We had a ganger from Hinton. She used to come around and say, 'does anyone want any work?' And that's how we got the work. We'd go up the road and get picked up from the caravan site off Hoarwithy Road. Oh, we had a laugh.

Lil Hopkins, 84, was born in Malvern, one of 11 children, third from the bottom. She has been around hops all her life. Her father George Gwynne was the trusted dryer at The Farm, Bosbury. He was gassed in the First World War and later in life became a cobbler, when working in the hot kiln conditions became too much for him. Whenever they could, Lil and husband George worked together:

> George did the stringing and I always braced behind him. The kids were small, and I had to go out to work, you had to in those days. We used to earn money like that. We called it piece-work. I could earn a day's money in half a day and then I could go home. I didn't like bracing behind anyone else other than George. They would do it too loose see.

Clockwise from top left: Dudley hop-tyers at Millend, 1975 (© George Hopkins); Training hops at Little Lambswick (© Edie Pound); Tyers at Little Lambswick, 1960s (© Roger Bray); Barbara and Graham Andrews bracing, 1984 (© Andrews family); Tyers at Hall Court, Rushall (© Doreen Pocknell); Gladys Fluck tying hops at Deans Place (© Pete Cotton)

Gladys Barnett, born in 1925, was another child of the hops, brought up at Castle Frome, surrounded by yards as far as the eye could see. Today there are just a handful of hopyards, whilst, in her youth, there were dozens. She still yearned for them decades after she last set foot inside one. Her father was a wagoner and the family grew their own vegetables, kept chickens and of course a family pig. Just as her mother had gone hop-tying before her, so Gladys did the same. There was no question about it. It was assumed:

> I worked on a hop farm after I married John Barnett, who was a wireworker, and tied hops there. I thoroughly enjoyed it. I'd go now if I could. My heart is still there. It's the smell, it catches you. But hop work was backbreaking because I couldn't sit on the floor or kneel, so had to bend over all day. It made you tired, but it was rewarding to look around and see a hopyard that looked like a row of nettles when you went in to do some tying and, when you went home at night, you'd done one row or two, and it was nice to look back and see these tidy things grow. And we spent the rest of the summer, after you'd tied them, twiggling them up with sticks, round the strings, until they were picked. As they grew, we used a stick to get them training up the string.

Edward Lewis, supplier of hop-growing essentials, standing in front of balls of coir at his warehouse (© Marsha O'Mahony)

Since it takes some 15-miles of coir per acre of hops, hundreds of poles and thousands of hooks and pegs, and dried hops from those yards were packed into countless hop pockets, the numbers of items needed for hop growing were mind-boggling, and proprietors of hop growers' requisites enjoyed good business. But as the industry has shrunk, so have their numbers. Edward Lewis bears the vicissitudes of hop growing with a rueful smile. From his warehouse he supplies growers all over the country (including newcomer to hop growing, the Eden Project in Cornwall), with everything they could possibly want or dream of. His warehouse is stacked high with pegs, wire, coir, pockets, socks (into which bales are packed), stencils, monkeys, poles – you name it, Edward supplies it. He has witnessed first-hand the seismic changes in the industry. When he started in the late-1960s there were 1,200 growers:

> Hops was a huge industry and the amount of labour involved was quite staggering. It is shrinking. But it's significant to us here and to other places. But as soon as you think you've got it right, it will bite you in the butt. Every year is a different year. But that's hop growing for you.

Edward sources poles from Archangel in north-west Russia; needles for stitching the hop pockets came from the dying needle industry in Redditch; wire from Luxembourg, redirected to city of steel Sheffield for stranding (stranded wire is composed of a number of small wires bundled together and is more

Simon Parker sewing a hop pocket at Instone Court (© Laura Haworth)

flexible than solid wire); and balls of coir, made from coconut husks, imported from Sri Lanka. The bureaucratic hoops Edward has to jump through these days to import coir is headache-inducing: 'It used to be just a couple of phone calls.' Not any more.

The jute hop pockets, into which dried hops were pressed, so emblematic of the hop, are falling out of fashion; baling dried hops is where it's all at these days. Edward still supplies pockets. There are one or two who still use them, but most of his customers now use socks as they move towards baling hops. The grower's name is still stencilled on and Edward is certain he has a stencil for every farm in his warehouse. It was all done in-house at one time and all his family have been recruited at one time or another, to help in the stencilling production line. 'We used to have little rollers, like paint rollers, and would use ink. When the children got older, they used to help out. We did 10,000 here one year. That was all through the summer.'

Simon Parker stencilling a hop pocket at Instone Court (© Laura Haworth)

In the 1920s, A.E. Walker of Tenbury, offered rock-bottom prices with the added promise of having 'coir yarn wound on the premises'. It was all in-house at Thinghill Court: string came in big bales and a group of women spooled them into balls using a machine turned by a handle. Philip Price's mother was one of them: 'You'd get the skeins, like skeins of wool, put them on like a turning table, and run it up to the machine and keep turning the handle 'til it got filled up. The string went around and round until it was full and into a ball. All by hand.'

The family-run industry continued at Bishops Frome for the Lewis family when 300-weight bales arrived in hanks. According to Edward Lewis: 'We would stick the bale, like a big skein, on this little roundabout and feed that into the baller. Then the Sri Lankans got the idea of balling it themselves, which was cheaper, and that was that. Didn't have to do it anymore.'

There was some help at hand, however, from the unlikeliest of places: Worcester Prison. In December 1903 *The Worcestershire Chronicle* featured the annual report from the Governor of Worcester Prison. He had taken time to demonstrate to the good citizens of the city the gainful employment of his inmates. He wrote:

> The discipline of the prison is very satisfactory. There are 248 male prisoners and 76 females. The system of earning remission by good work and conduct is an excellent thing and I think might, with advantage, be extended to those whose sentences are of three-months or over. The conduct of the prisoners has been good on the whole, the majority of reports being for idleness, but no one would expect much else from the class of men, tramps and loafers who incur them. There have been no escapes or attempts to escape, and no case of corporal punishment. Male prisoners have been employed making mats, rugs, nose bags and mail bags, coir bailing and sack making.

The Bushel – the bushel basket emporiums

A bushel = a dry measurement of capacity equal to eight gallons (36 litres)

The word bushel is synonymous with the hop. The bushel basket, invariably made in numerous cottage-like industries across the rural landscape, was the basic measure of the hopyard. The average bushel, however, was subject to slippage according to one Horsham grower: 'The bushel was a standard measurement, but each county had its own standard and sometimes each farm had its own standard! Baskets were made free-hand, and there were no moulds or anything like that. Someone probably just sat there with it between their knees and thought, "that looks about right"!'

Demand for the raw material grew, according to a 1911 report in *The Ross Gazette* describing the establishment of 'new osier plantations to meet the demands of basket and crate makers'. A fruit merchant described the correct construction of a bushel in a letter to the *Hereford Times* in December 1911: 'A well-made bushel costs about 1s; wicker made with 3 cane bindings round the rim. The life of a bushel is about 4 to 5 years'. Mr Tom Ellison is one name amongst a legion of basket makers and bushel weavers. His work, on display at the Three Counties Show in the summer of 1956, made a clean sweep of the wickerwork section. He started as an apprentice in 1913, at the age of 13, to a Hampton basket maker. Mr Ellison served in the Navy during the Second World War, but was released on medical grounds in 1942, and, because he could only carry on light work, he returned to basket-making. Aside from weaving baskets for the busheller, this gentleman wove baskets for pigeons, fishing, dogs, eggs, fruit and, curiously, a baby's rattle.

Clockwise from above left: Peeling osiers for baskets (© Miss White); Basket-maker, Brampton Abbotts (© Heather Hurley/ Landscape Origins of the Wye Project); Cutting withies (© Miss Wight)

4

Picking the Hop:
the pickers

*I came to Ledbury in 1944 when my father was appointed foreman for E.B. &
D.H. Thompson hop growers. We came from Leicestershire and Dad's new boss
got us permits to move our furniture on the railway. It took us a week to move.
My sister and I thought we were going to a foreign land. It was a large farm,
800 acres, 16 men, two boys and three pairs of horses and three tractors. They
still tell the tale today of how Dad had never seen a hop before and didn't know
how they grew! The men could not understand that there were folks who lived
without hops – we soon learned to live with them!*

WI Herefordshire, *Within Living Memory*, 1993

Hop picking was a period of such short and high intensity that the
days of the hand-picked harvest have left their stamp on the collective
memory, becoming the stuff of legend, lore and myth passed down the
family line. It brought an unprecedented pilgrimage of people to these
three counties, biblical in scale and drama, an exodus from the industrial
centres. Growers were delighted to see them arrive and equally delighted to
see them leave. They came on foot, by bike, horse and cart, caravan, char-
abanc, train, truck and even boat. Their appearance transformed hitherto
sleepy, in some cases backwater, rural communities, into hives and bustles
of activity, and often licentiousness. In the early part of the twentieth
century, the *Midland Gospel Mission to the Hop Pickers of Herefordshire and
Worcestershire* was just one of several organisations dedicated to their welfare. It was calculated then that 40,000 people left their Midlands homes
for the harvest. The numbers were further swelled by thousands more from
South Wales, the Forest of Dean, Manchester, Ellesmere and, of course,
from the Gypsy community. The ripple effect on the local economy was

substantial. Without this rag-taggle mob, there would have been no harvest, and no beer. The revolution brought about by the arrival of the hop-picking machine after the Second World War changed everything, bringing an end to this fairy-tale era.

There was an air of expectancy, and some dread too, as the picking season approached. Things were about to change for the next month or so. For Janet Parker and her sister Mary at The Sponend, their Fromes Hill home in the 1940s, it was a time of unparalleled excitement:

> Our pickers came mainly from Worcester. Dad used to fetch them in our lorry and Mary and I couldn't wait to meet some of the families who came year after year. Mrs Sutton was our ganger lady and she was the person who agreed the price of a bushel of hops with Dad. We also had local people from Fromes Hill. I still meet a lady who recalls our picking days as the happiest of her life. At weekends the husbands used to come out on the bus from Worcester to visit. They usually ended up at the local pub, the Wheatsheaf, and had a beer or two and usually came back singing. Oliver Howe was the landlord then and he had a shop too where he used to keep a mousetrap on the counter by the cheese!

For many, coming from the industrial heartlands, pale and often undernourished, their arrival in this rural idyll was like arriving in paradise. Peter Davies at Claston described their transformation, especially the children. After several weeks picking, they became freckled, tanned and heartily sustained with good country food and air. It's little wonder the pickers returned year after year. John Hosie was a Glasgow schoolboy in the 1930s. At harvest time, he was sent to stay with his grandmother, who lived in a farm labourer's cottage in a hamlet near Ashperton. He gives a lovely account of a city boy's arrival in the hop heartlands:

> At Glasgow Central Station, my Mother would select a compartment which a family occupied and ask them to keep an eye on me. With my suitcase and pack of sandwiches placed on the rack above and a small bottle of home-made lemonade for the journey, my mother would have a word with the guard and firmly impress on me the need to take care of my ticket. When I arrived at Hereford at 6.00pm Uncle Albert was

The *Hereford Times* reports the arrival of hop pickers at Ashperton in 1952

waiting for me. I remember the long wait for the train to Stoke Edith station (*see overleaf*). It will always remain in my memory. I can still see the station gardens with all the flowers in bloom and the pink rambling roses that threaded their way along the railings. The porter would come running to collect our tickets and we waited for the train to puff out of the station before we could cross the line. Uncle Albert would strap my suitcase to his bicycle and then it was forward to where my grandmother lived. I would breathe in the fresh air that was so foreign to me, see the hedgerows with all the wild flowers and the birds singing their last songs of the evening. We veered off under the Little Tarrington railway bridge into fields, over stiles and along paths through orchards full of cider apple trees and hopyards in the distance. Finally, there were the lights of the cottage shining in the distance – it had been a long journey for me.

Edwardian hop pickers at Stoke Edith station, early twentieth century (© Derek Foxton)

Closer to home, but no less exciting a journey, Jeanette Bates (née Read) travelled from Hereford to Dents of Yarkhill in the 1930s. Her picture of life in the hopyard is equally vivid and evocative:

> We used to get up at 6.30am, in the middle of the night for us kids, but we soon got used to it. A quick breakfast and off to catch the bus. Oh, how I hated waiting for the bus. We had to wear our oldest clothes and I thought everyone walking by was looking at us! But once we were in the hop fields, we were all dressed the same. We would be taken to our house of hops where there would be a crib for us to pick into. The first job was to pull the bines down and a man with a long pole would do that, the pole puller. Sometimes my brother would swing on them. We used to hope that they were big hops and fill the crib quicker. We children were given an open brolly, turned upside down, to pick into. Once that was full, we were allowed to light the fire with sticks we found in the fields. The smell of that fire with the kettle boiling for tea was wonderful. I can still smell it now.

Early twentieth-century photo by Alfred Watkins, of children picking hops into upturned umbrellas (© HARC)

The highlight of the day was when the Humbug Man appeared at the gate. He had walked from Hereford with his little brown case full of humbugs. These were delicious pieces of transparent toffee on a stick. I've never tasted anything so gorgeous since. Mind you, we were only allowed one if we had been good. The journey home was lovely – happy memories as we motored along the country lanes, singing. The bus would drop us off, tired and dirty, and once home it was a good wash to get the stains and smell of hops from our hands. A quick supper and off to bed to dream of Gene Kelly. Those were the days.

Bishops Frome epitomised the influx and similar scenes were played out in other villages across Herefordshire, Shropshire and Worcestershire. Bishops Frome's population swelled from just 700 to over 5,000. One account compares the village, seen from Fromes Hill, to that of a medieval encampment, the quiet hum of people and camp-fires dotted across the landscape, balladry and singing providing background music. It was said that if you could not get a job in Bishops Frome at harvest time, then you couldn't get one anywhere. Accommodation in the village for W.F. Pudge's pickers early in the 1900s was described as Tin Town. Most growers provided similar accommodation,

Hop pickers' tents with hop kilns beyond (© Derek Evans/ HARC)

Gypsy vardoes parked in The Southend, Ledbury (Alfred Watkins © Herefordshire Libraries)

barracks of varying comfort; sheds, pigsties, cow barns, all, with any luck, cleaned out and whitewashed, but not always so. The Gypsy community were self-sufficient, arriving in their gleaming caravans, often camped away from other pickers, their colourful cavalcade watched with wonder, curiosity and some trepidation. Pickers arriving from towns and cities came prepared. Some went as far as bringing along basic furniture, chairs, tables and, in some circumstances, even going to the effort of applying wallpaper to their basic accommodation. Housewives kept a special hopping box in the months leading up to the picking season, something like a tea chest, into which went tins or packets of food, supplies for their hop excursion.

FROM TANDEMS TO TRAINS, CARTS TO CHARABANCS –
GETTING TO THE HOPYARDS

It was like the arrival of a fair or a circus: the anticipation, the noise, the clatter, the spectacle, the groundswell of bodies. The logistics of getting pickers to and from the farms and hopyards were immense, often organised, sometimes a shambles and occasionally creative. Hop-pickers' train specials were laid on from South Wales, the Midlands and beyond. At just one small station, Withington, 2,000 pickers crammed the platforms ready for the next stage of their journey. Accommodating the pickers was one of the reasons cited for the opening of the Worcester to Leominster line in 1874. Growers engaged every haulage company going or used their own trucks. It seems anything with wheels was commandeered. Mary Trenchard-Morgan's father grew hops at Kimbolton and collected his pickers from Leominster in the back of his horse box. Lesley Whistance of Garway was unusual in being one of the few women drivers, bringing pickers down from the Black Country.

Hop pickers arriving at the Leys, Tarrington (photo by A.W. Zimmerman © Derek Foxton)

They left an impression:

> It was an annual event, collecting a very friendly, happy bunch of people from the Wren's Nest Pub in Dudley. They used this pub as a rendezvous to meet the bus. They loaded tea chests with all their food and cooking utensils for their hop-picking holiday. These were pushed into the bus aisle and in the storage cupboards along the bus sides. Dudley folk of all ages, male and female, young and old. A 50-ish woman, curly-haired, stocky, was the boss. She made sure everyone, and all the belongings, were on board. She was their mouthpiece too and talked all the way to Bromyard. Their destination was Munderfield for Mr and Mrs Charles. When they finished there, they all moved on to Mrs Payne's at Canon Frome. Then we did the return journey to Wren's Nest. Everyone agreed with the boss lady that it had been the most marvellous holiday and especially good because they were returning home with money in their pockets.

Old Hill hop pickers (© The Black Country Living Museum)

Frank Nicklin was one of those who was waiting at the Wren's Nest. Like many Dudley families, the Nicklins went hop picking every year to Bennetts at Slatch Farm, Bosbury:

> We would pack our hop-picking box and take it to the Wren's Nest pub on the night before we were due to go. There were no vandals then, and a couple of blokes would stack them ready to be picked up the next morning. The journey was through Worcester, Malvern, Colwall and Bosbury. When we arrived, we were greeted by Mr Bennett, a typical farmer, well-built, breeches, boots with gaiters, and a red face, a very healthy-looking man.

Black Country Bugle

Charles Pudge's family have been growing hops at Frogend, Bishops Frome for ten generations. The Pudges – like the Parkers, the Andrews, the Walkers, the Adams, the Hawkins, the Morrises – are hop dynasties. Charles' father John had his hands full with 500 pickers descending on his land:

> Father used to send three buses to the Black Country and Frome Valley transport lorries and when they were coming they didn't carry anything, and their cases were light. But when they left to go back home, well, you wanted a winch to get their cases back on, they were that full of potatoes and apples!

Frome Valley Transport (*see p. 207*), based in Bishops Frome, was one of the biggest hauliers of hops in the district. Its eminent logistics skills came in handy too when its trucks and drivers were called upon to bring pickers – and their luggage – to and from the hopyards. Philip Bowler, owner of Frome Valley Transport, was kept very busy:

> We used to pick up the hop pickers' luggage from the Black Country and from the Welsh valleys. They had all their cases and boxes with their clothes, but there were also the odd few tables and chairs and that sort of stuff. It was always well organised. When you went up for the luggage, the farmer always had a someone, usually a lady, who had recruited the pickers, and you would report to her when you got up there with the truck. And often her husband would get in the lorry and he knew which streets the luggage was waiting to be collected and loaded up. It would be piled up on the pavement ready for collection. You didn't have to wait. It was there ready.

Pickers even came by boat. In October 1911 the journey of a group from Wolverhampton warranted a mention in the *Worcester Journal* after a fracas interrupted their return home. They had been picking hops at Holt Fleet and were travelling to Stourport by boat on the River Severn. After motoring upstream, they alighted at Stourport and headed for the train station for carriage to Wolverhampton, where the fight erupted. They were fined five shillings each and told to make their way home.

Lulham Court head wagoner Harry Warburton (*left*) with Granville Powell, Charlie Green and hop pickers including Mrs Turpin and Mrs Mole, both in their nineties (© Charles Green)

Rosemary Armishaw, Elsie Heath, Mary Morris and Joyce Harper picking hops at Hawkins Farm, Withington in the 1940s (© Herefordshire Lore)

Farm labourers at Millend (© George and Lil Hopkins)

In the pre-Second World War years, Thomas Fielding and his family and friends walked to Ledbury from Gloucester on foot over two days, sleeping in hedges, fortified with cider, cheese and bread. At the end of the harvest, they returned home, also on foot.

John Ridgway, 83, is a retired upholsterer from Hereford. During the war years, living in Tupsley, Hereford, he picked hops with his mother at Dormington. A lorry picked them and other families up from the end of Hampton Dean Road. The lorry had some benches in the back if they were lucky – luckier still if there were straw bales. His aunt and uncle, however, travelled up from their South Wales' home:

> My uncle was a miner, and this was their holiday. They came up on
> his motorbike and side-car. Back home he had to get it down a narrow
> passageway, so he unbolted it first. When he got it to the front of the
> house he joined it together again. Then he and his wife loaded the bike
> up ready for their journey to the hopyard at Dormington. When he was
> happy he hadn't forgotten anything, he put his foot down on the pedal,
> and shot off. It was some minutes later and some distance down the road
> before he noticed his wife was still in the side-car – back home!

Above and opposite: hop picking at Dormington in the 1940s
(all © Derek Foxton/ Tony Williams Collection)

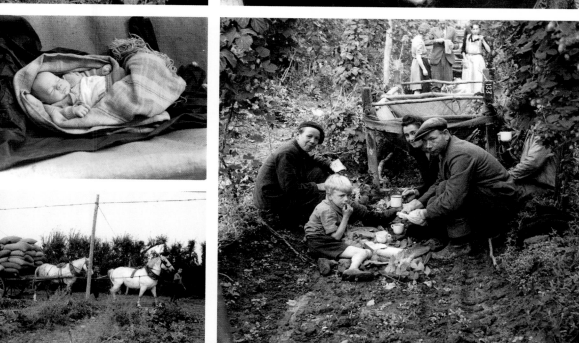

Some pickers, however, didn't even get started, waylaid along the way for various reasons. In 1955 Margaret Kelly, 64, was on her way to pick hops at Ledbury but didn't make it further than Monmouth, where she was arrested and thrown into the 'local prison for being drunk and disorderly and doing damage in the borough.' (*Monmouth Beacon*, 1955). She had form though, with 105 previous convictions.

There was no age limit to being a hop picker. In September 1956 Mrs Emily Ibell was interviewed in the *Ross Gazette* from her hop-picking stool at Upton Court, Upton Bishop. At the age of 93, she was in her 66th year of hop picking, so she was a relatively late-starter to the delights of the hop harvest. In her prime she picked 20 bushels a day, starting work at 6.30am every morning, 'the hops weighed up better when the dew was on them', she observed. Before marriage, and when Queen Victoria was on the throne, she 'went abroad' and worked in Dulwich, in service for a certain Mr W.H. Smith, of 'the well-known stationers'. One of her sons died as a result of being a prisoner in the First World War. Leaving Mrs Ibell to continue her picking, the reporter reassured the reader that she 'retains all her faculties'.

The collection point for many Leominster pickers was by the solitary tree at the back of the old Clifton cinema. Pickers for Brierley Court were collected there in a First World War Morris one-ton lorry, canvas covering the back. Alec Haines often helped: 'It didn't have modern things like a starter, but a magneto and I had to start it with a handle at the front. At Brierley there's a very steep bank and sometimes in low gear it wouldn't go up and I would have to reverse and ask for 10 or 15 people to get off. I drove that darned thing for four years.'

Picking at Bromyard
(© John Symonds)

There were treats for some who went to collect pickers from the Black Country. Sheila Pinches went to Dudley with her grandfather, hop grower Albert Hancocks, of Wyercroft, Bishops Frome: 'We went in an old army lorry to collect the hop pickers and many of them were workers in the local sweet factory. They always used to give me a tin of sweets from the factory whenever we picked them up.'

The singing voices of Welsh pickers feature in many memories. Doreen Thomas remembered them:

bursting into song at any opportunity. Sometimes they would fight amongst themselves, and at other times they would sing beautifully. You never really knew what you were going to get! They always seemed to be singing when they got off the trucks. When I was about ten my mother was asked to be the leader of our bus. It was a Yeomans bus, and I felt very important. The journey to the hopyard was the best, with everyone singing at the top of their voices. If you were in a yard where the hops were not very good the leaders of the buses, together with the leaders of the Welsh pickers, would all go and talk to the farmer and get him to pay more. There would be even more singing after that.

A Yeomans bus, c.1950s (© Michael Griffith)

Albert Hancocks collected pickers for his crop as well as for his relatives at nearby Cusop Farm. His great-grandson Rob, still growing hops, recalls a story passed down the family line:

He used to go and fetch them on an old army lorry because everybody had an old army truck then. On their journey home, the pickers would have ransacked a few apples. When the lorries were going through the centre of Worcester, the young boys used to throw apples at people on the streets!

Reg Bayliss was a drover at Hereford Livestock Market for over 50 years. When he was interviewed in 2006, he had been a haulage driver for 70 years with never an accident. With his son Peter, he hauled hop pockets for dozens of growers. But they also had the entertainment of collecting pickers:

> We used to go down to South Wales on a Saturday or a Sunday with a stock lorry – that's all we had, nothing fancy. They used to get in the lorry and bring bits of furniture with them, their bed and sideboards, stools, that sort of thing. It was a holiday for them. They used to walk from Rosemaund up to the Crozen Arms, and when they came back at night, the singing was fantastic, 'cause they were well-oiled by then. You'd always hear them coming and they were singing in full voice. It was lovely.

Gypsy children, with vardoes in the background, at Claston Farm, Dormington, where hand-picking ended in 1957 (© Derek Evans/ HARC)

A member of the Smith
family of Gypsies
(© The Smith family/
Herefordshire Lore)

The arrival of the Gypsy cavalcade was much anticipated, its appearance
often marking the beginning of the hop harvest. Gypsies were a valued part
of the labour force during the hand-picking days, a formidable picking force:
quick, hard-working, often there at first light before anyone else, and still
there when others had packed up at the end of the day.

Traveller Mike Johns lives in Ledbury, but as a youngster he travelled from
farm to farm in the family's bow-top wagon during the season:

> Father built the wagon himself, all the travellers did then, starting with a
> flat four-wheel dray and building it from there. We used to do the Much
> Cowarne Farm and Paske's of Bromyard and then down to Burley Gate.
> There is an old oak tree there and I can still picture granddad standing
> under it with all the barrel top and open wagons around. They were
> good days.

TIN TOWN, TENTS, CARAVANS, BARNS AND BUSES –
PICKERS' ACCOMMODATION

Pigsties, barns, tin sheds and tents – all, at one time or another, provided accommodation for pickers. In the weeks leading up to the pickers' arrival, preparations for these temporary living conditions began: scrubbing, sweeping out, whitewashing, supplying boultings of straw. Toilet facilities were a rarity. For now, it was a case of finding a quiet corner in the hopyard and crouching down. Water was fetched in Corona bottles or buckets from the pump, stream, well or from the farmer's wife. Some barracks were of a higher standard than others, leading some pickers to complain, and some local authorities to express concern. Nonetheless, the pickers kept on coming; it didn't put anyone off.

During the 1938 season, the *Hereford Times* reported on Mr G. Davies of Avenbury, Bromyard. He was cross at criticism aimed at the growers and their poor accommodation provision: 'Farmers really cannot afford furnished apartments with feather beds for hop pickers', he harrumphed.

Above left: tented accommodation for hop pickers (© Brian Willder)

Above right: Tedney footbridge over the River Teme, used by pickers to reach their accommodation (© Peter Walker)

Left: Advert from 1900, for hop pickers' bedding supplies (*Bromyard News*)

FOR HOP-PICKERS.

GOOD WARM SHEETS, 2/6, 3/3, 3/4, per pair.
HURDEN SHEETS, 2/11, 3/11, 4/11, „
GOOD HEAVY BLANKETS,
            3/3, 4/3, 4/11, 5/11, „
WARM BED QUILTS, 2/4, 2/11, 3/9 each.
CRIB CLOTH in every Width and Quality.

Yet Charles Pudge, as a boy, saw first-hand some of the pickers' homes:

> I can remember going up to the Black Country; father had three gangers
> up there. We went to Willenhall first to this house and he said, "you are
> not to have anything to eat or drink in these houses unless I do". So, he's
> talking to this old couple and I was fascinated by these beetles in the
> house. It took me another 30 years to work out they were cockroaches.
> There were no internal doors, there were no bannisters, there were no
> front of the stairs, some of the door jammers were missing. It's still the
> only house I have ever been to where the coal was in the bath.

Describing his 'holiday' to Shelsey Walsh to pick hops in 1950, Birmingham
boy, Graham Paul Webb, describes deprivation that would make you weep:

> For hop picking I had no clothes or shoes that were worthy of that name,
> and certainly no underpants. My ragged shorts were hand-me-downs
> from my older brothers and were only held up by string that was normally
> used to train hop vines. My mum, a war widow with five kids and a pride
> that was bigger than her family, only accepted help once in her life and
> that was a pair of army hobnail boots for my bare feet. They were far too
> big for me and I had no socks. I would traipse up and down the hopyards
> all day and the boots rubbed all the skin off and the inevitable happened
> and I got an infection. There were always nuns going up and down the
> hop fields trying to convert us heathens from our evil ways. I think it was
> one of them that realised how serious my condition was and I was rushed
> to Brum for an emergency operation. After that I was shipped back to
> Shelsey Walsh where my family was still hop picking and the nuns would
> come around daily to change my dressings.
>
> *Birmingham History Forum*

A Great Western Railway rule book from 1936 was unrepentant in its treatment of hop pickers. In an appendix titled, 'Coaches for Conveyance of Hop
Pickers', it states, 'Only THIRD-class coaches of the oldest type must be
used for the conveyance of hop pickers. In no circumstances are lavatory
carriages or carriages with first-class compartments to be provided'.

Hop Barracks

During hop picking some pickers would camp in tents or – particularly in the case of the many Gypsies who went hop picking – sleep in the caravans they arrived in. Others would be put up in existing farm buildings (including those with a loft floor or 'tallet'). Others still were housed in purpose-built outbuildings known as barracks. These were often rudimentary structures, single-storey, clad and roofed in corrugated iron. The barracks might be sub-divided into single dormitory rooms, each with its own door and window. Some had a communal eating area at one end, with a fireplace for cooking. Because of their humble character and insubstantial construction, these shack-like buildings are relatively rare survivals, and unlikely to be protected in the ways that other historically significant building types are. They often survive in locations where the adjacent hopyards are long gone, robbing them of their meaningful context.

ROSS UNION RURAL SANITARY AUTHORITY.

PUBLIC HEALTH ACT, 1875.
(38 & 39 Vict. c. 55. s. 314.)

BYELAWS
FOR

Securing the decent Lodging and Accommodation of Persons engaged in Hop-picking.

We, the Guardians of the Poor of the Ross Union, in the Counties of Hereford and Gloucester, being the Rural Sanitary Authority for the district of the said Union, do make and ordain the following byelaws for regulating the decent lodging and accommodation of persons engaged in hop-picking in the district :—

Habitations to which byelaws apply.

I.—The following byelaws shall be applicable to all tents, sheds, barns, hopper-houses, buildings or other habitations appropriated and used from time to time, for the lodging of persons engaged in hop-picking ; provided the byelaw sshall not extend to any building occupied as a dwelling house, or for human habitation, from time to time throughout the year.

Construc-tion,ventila-tion, and lighting of habitations.

II.—Every person using any such habitation for the lodging of persons engaged in hop-picking shall cause it to be constructed and maintained so that it may be thoroughly clean, dry, and waterproof at all times when used for the lodging of such persons. He shall cause such habitation in every case to be properly ventilated, and where practicable sufficiently lighted.

Allowance of floor space.

III.—No such person shall cause or allow a greater number of adult persons to be received into any such habitation, or any room therein, at any one time, for the purpose of sleeping therein, than may be compatible with the allowance of 16 square feet, at the least, of available floor space in respect of each adult person.
For the purpose of the foregoing·provision two children under 10 years of age may be counted as one adult.

Provision of screens for beds.

IV.—Every such person shall cause every room or part of such habitation, which may be appropriated for the reception of adult persons of different sexes, to be so furnished and provided that every bed shall be properly separated from any adjoining bed by a suitable screen or partition, of such material, construction, and size as to secure adequate privacy to the occupant or occupants of such bed.

Cooking-houses.

V.—Every such person shall provide in a safe and suitable position in, or in connexion with, or adjacent to such habita-tion, a suitable cooking-house, or other place, properly covered or sheltered, in which fires may be safely and readily lighted, and food may be properly cooked, and clothes and other articles may be properly dried. He shall cause such cooking-house or place to be so constructed that for every 15 persons authorised to be received in such habitation a separate fireplace or separate accommodation for the cooking of food, and the drying of clothes and other articles, may be provided.

First five clauses of the 1875 byelaws for hop-pickers' accommodation (© HARC)

Hop pickers'
barracks at
Bidney, near
Dilwyn
(© R. Wheeler)

Hop pickers'
barracks near
Ashperton,
erected by
F.H. Dale of
Leominster
(© R. Wheeler)

Hop pickers'
barracks at
Dormington
(© R. Wheeler)

Gladys Barnett's father fetched pickers fresh off the train from Dudley at Ashperton Station and transported them by horse and wagon to their barracks. With her mother, Gladys helped prepare their accommodation:

> We used to whitewash them out a bit and the men used to put straw for bedding. Some of the better-off ones had things they used to put on it, otherwise it was just blankets. In August mum and Mrs Hopkins used to wash the blankets and peg them out in the field to dry in time for September when the picking began. Basically, the pickers roughed it.

Newspapers were generous with their linage on stories from the hop fields: there was a lot going on and a lot to report. Some of the tales tragic, others baffling, more hilarious. In October 1954 Mrs Maude Matthews was lucky to survive a fire that swept through the hop-picker's quarters at Whitehouse Farm, Canon Frome. The widow lost all her possessions. Hop pickers attacked the flames with buckets of water until the fire brigade arrived. Frustratingly, she listed her losses with no explanation: 'I have lost everything, including my hop-picking money. And another thing, my daughter's wedding dress in which she was recently married, all destroyed!'

In Shropshire, Ray Morris' workforce came from the Black Country:

> We had local ones too and then pickers from Dudley and West Bromwich. They came by their hundreds by train to Tenbury Wells Station and one of our workmen would go with a horse and cart or, a bit later on, the old Standard Fortune, to bring them here. They lived in the buildings out there and their menfolk used to come at the weekends, but it was havoc then. They were forever scrumping apples to take back. But it was all part of it.

While part of this army arrived on buses, hop grower Neil Parker solved an accommodation problem by having his pickers sleep in some. He purchased two double-deckers from Hereford Yeomans bus services, towed them back to his farm, put in electric lights and two compartments, upstairs and down, partitioned them, put down some straw and provided blankets. But there was one problem: 'The Council said we needed to have actual beds, so I bought 30 from the Army & Navy stores near Leominster and put straw on top of them; they were £1 each!'

The remarks column in the Ankerdine hop-picking ledger for 1922, detailing an incident of scrumping, with two men being 'collared' by the local sergeant (© Peter Walker)

MAKE WAY FOR THE PICKERS

The good, the bad, the ugly, the industrious, the desperate, the lazy, the poor, the rich, the old, the young – they all came with their various needs, reasons and requirements. New friendships formed, relationships blossomed, feuding factions simmered against the backdrop of middle England's countryside, fortified by fresh air, good food and the occasional beer or cider. The annual influx even presented some linguistic challenges. Joseph Lewey picked up a Herefordshire accent while he worked at Leighton Court and on visits back home no one could understand him. In Leominster, Welsh speakers pouring over the border prompted some observers to comment that, 'English has stopped being the dominant language in Leominster and official notices are being posted in Welsh as well as English'.

Neil Parker struggled to make sense of his hop pickers:

For the first week or so I didn't know what they were saying, and then after a while I started talking like them! We had one old girl who was clearly in charge from Bootle, quite a character. Dad used to write to her and say how many men he wanted and how many women. She picked the price that we paid them per hour. You didn't argue. She was also a money lender and used to lend money out in the week for them to go up to the pub. She charged an extortionate amount.

John Probert of Church House Farm, Weston Beggard, led a full life, driven by his passions: family, friends, fun, farming and 'flipping hops'. As a teenager helping his father with the bushelling, he experienced a tongue-lashing from a Black Country picker he was never to forget. His son, Tom, included it in his father's eulogy: 'He was trying to keep the hop pickers' children off the sacks of bushelled hops. One of the mothers didn't like it, she was quite formidable, and threatened him with, "if yow do that to arr kid again, I'll shake the shite outta yow!"'

PUBS AND INNS

Local pubs did excellent business during the picking season. It was bounty time for the brewing industry, although one memorable picker got her tipple not from the pub, but the chemist. Neil Parker:

> Old Mrs Greer drank meths. She always had a drop at the end of her nose. It was blue. A good worker though. One time she went to the chemist in Bromyard and asked for a bottle of meths. He realised what was going on and said, "I'm sorry, we've run out". To which she replied, "how about a bottle of surgical spirit then?" Again, "sorry, I've run out of that too". She wasn't happy. "Call yourself a bloody chemist," she said.

The Five Bridges pub, popular with hop pickers, here visited by a local bobby (© Tom Nellist)

Hop pickers from Wootton, Checkley (© Stuart Cooper)

At Newtown Crossroads, Russell Bunn's father was landlord at the New Inn, the setting for some riotous evenings during the picking season. Similar scenes played out in pubs across hop-growing districts, a profitable time for publicans. The New Inn was surrounded by hopyards – Woodmanton, Cowarne Court, Whittick Manor, Monksbury Court, Eggleton – which provided a captive audience for the pub. Russell, 93, farms at Checkley but his boyhood days were spent at Newtown. Many of his relations lived and farmed in the parish, and he used to help with hay-making. One of his jobs was to bring cider to men in the fields. He tried it of course and ended by sleeping off the effects in a ditch.

This was tame in comparison to the ebullient clientele at the New Inn:

On a Sunday night they used to come with their wives and children. In some cases they didn't have proper shoes on. They'd run around in bare feet. We couldn't keep up with the orders. We would open the beer taps into a tin bath and customers used anything at hand, jam jars, tea cups, tins, anything to make up their pint of beer, dip them in the bath and pay the money. You'd come out the following morning and find bodies along the road. They'd be gone a few hours later.

Horse sales happened on some Sunday mornings. One former grower used to visit his Gypsy pickers out of season at their Bristol base. He was very fond of them:

> The best workers. Every Sunday morning they would congregate at the local pubs, the Bell at Bosbury, the Oak at Stapelow, other pubs at Ashperton and Bishops Frome, and then go horse-dealing. Get boozed up, riders trotting up and down the road, saddle-less, potential buyers looking from the side lines, stroking and checking the horse. It made life very complicated I can tell you! There was always one woman in charge, wearing a long black skirt. When a deal was done the cash would go down her front somewhere!

Members of the Nelson Gypsy family at Dormington Court (© David Warnes)

The Boxbush pub at Ashperton – now closed – was the location for some raucous scenes as deals were made and lost. John Barnett:

Every third Sunday in hop picking the Gypsies used to hold their horse fairs there. There was a landlady there, a widow, and she used to serve out through the window into the yard. The Gypsies used to buy horses and sell them, and traps and things like that. It was really big. And they would fight too. Well to be honest, the locals used to try and get them going. And when it started, it was brilliant, the ring of people used to form. As the fight moved across the road then the ring would move too! And the police would stand about 60 yards down the road and never bat an eyelid. There wasn't much they could have done.

Two young men from the Locke family in Shropshire (© Bill Kerswell)

Growers often relied on an individual, most often a woman – an indomitable, strong, no-nonsense type – to rally the workers in preparation for the harvest: the ganger. Granny Aldridge was the ganger at Moor Farm, Eardiston. Allegedly born in a hopyard, she was all of four-feet tall and a formidable character, who smoked a pipe and used rather colourful language. Margaret Wheatstone's mother, Edith, was a ganger for the Davies family at Claston:

She was a very strong woman. You did what you were told, no mistake about it. She was in charge. She used to say it was her fortnight's holiday, so we had a holiday, but we had to work for it. When I was a kid I had to fill an upside-down umbrella twice, then we were allowed to play. No leaves in them mind, you had to be a clean picker. Then you would stop for breakfast and lunch, right there by your crib, and light a fire. Mam had a green stool with three legs that Dad built for her and that was her table. As a ganger she didn't get paid more, just made sure the pickers were ok and got their money. She had a whistle mind, and if there was a strike she would blow it, shouting "everyone out!"

Gypsy hop pickers Amos Hoskins (*above*) and Beth Hoskins (*opposite*) (© Derek Evans/ HARC)

Pamela Powell was born in 1872 and was a ganger at Brierley Hill for farmer Grundy of Lower Hill Farm, Leominster. Her granddaughter, Gloria Smith, describes a hardworking woman and a tough life:

> Some 60 families would travel from Brierley Hill train station together with their tin boxes holding clothes, cooking utensils and food. When they arrived at Leominster they were all herded onto wagons, tin boxes first, then them on top and they would go away all singing and waving. Many of the women would go to the pub at night, but Granny would save her money and enjoy sitting around the camp-fire at night singing. She had no education, could not read or write, but she was a good business woman doing all her calculations on her fingers and she was never wrong. She ran a business back home in her kitchen making ginger beer and porter and selling faggots and peas to workmen. She was a good and generous person and a fine organiser for those hop-picking days.

The enticement of extra cash and country air was too much for some families who would defy the school truancy officer at hop-picking time. It sometimes resulted in a fine for a family that was already hovering on the poverty line.

Hop pickers, including many children, at Kyrewood in 1913 (© Andrew Lowe)

However, it seems the growers were complicit in this arrangement. In 1901, the *Worcestershire Chronicle* reported on a curious character, the 'Bellman', sent by hop growers to the back streets of industrial centres telling parents to defy School Boards, and 'if they were afterwards prosecuted, the hop growers will pay the fines!'

In the mid-1950s Monmouthshire Education Authority was vociferous in its pursuit of recalcitrant parents. One man was fined £4 for his wife and four children who had gone picking: 'She hasn't had a holiday in seven years', he said. The court was unmoved. At Blackwood, 18 parents were summoned for not sending their children to school in the picking season. One, a disabled ex-serviceman, had been summoned to court the previous four years and was fined £1 for each child.

Above: Hop pickers from Tupsley, including a number of school-age children, posing together in front of a crib (© John Ridgway)

Left: Young children in a hopyard (© Reginald Gaunt)

Above: Gypsy picker Pearly Butler and her daughter Rosie, at Claston Farm, Dormington, 1957.
Opposite: Children in the hopyard at Claston Farm (both © Derek Evans/ HARC)

THE BUSHELLER, THE BOOKER, THE BAGGER – COUNTING THE HOPS

The busheller could be intimidated mind. My father bushelled for 50 years, but he didn't want me to do it. He said it was the most unthankful job. Ray Morris, **Burton Mill Farm, Shropshire**

The busheller had a hard job and was often the least popular man in the yard. He measured the amount of hops picked with the bushel. Several times a day his arrival was announced with a cry of, 'bushel them up! bushel them up!,' or even 'clean them up! clean them up!' to urge pickers to remove leaves from the crib. By his side was the booker and the bagger. Into the crib he scooped the basket, emptying the hops into a sack held by the bagger, counting as he went, 'one, two, three'. The booker carefully marked each bushel in a notebook next to the picker's name, and the pickers kept their own record too. As the busheller worked, he was watched carefully. Was he a generous busheller, or a hard one? Was he going to press the contents down with an elbow, a most unpopular move, to get even more hops into the bushel? If so, it was likely to lead to some choice words, arguments or even punches thrown. It was not a job for the sensitive.

Busheller, bagger and booker measuring and recording hops picked (© Derek Evans/ HARC)

Top: Busheller and bagger at Carwardine (© John Griffiths). *Left*: POW bagger (© Brian Willder). *Above*: Bert Harris at Larport (© Mrs Janet Rowberry)

At Westhope, Mr Yeomans did the bushelling. 'If he were a bit heavy-handed these big hefty Welsh women would throw him into the crib with the hops. No one stood on great ceremony in those days, but everything was done in good spirit.' (Lynne Pugh, *Pyon Years: Memories of Life in the Parishes of Birley, Canon Pyon and King's Pyon 1900–1950s*, 2003).

In her youth, 94-year-old Mavis Harrison travelled with her family from Wales, catching the train to the Tram Inn at Allensmore, from where they walked to hopyards at Bridge Sollars, a ten-mile walk carrying luggage for the picking season. There was little affection for their busheller:

He used to bully the pickers by pushing his elbow in the basket, pressing the hops down, therefore fewer bushels for us, so they would have to pick more until they made any money. But a Gypsy man, picking with his family, noticed this and asked Mum to come and set up by them and stand by him. When the busheller tried his usual trick, the Gypsy man coughed and the busheller looked up. The Gypsy man told him he thought he had better look again, his hand pulling back his coat to reveal a huge knife (country people used knives for all sorts of things back in the 1930s). We had no trouble after that and made some wonderful friends in the Gypsy family who we would see year after year.

Neil Parker's brother bushelled at Hopton Sollars:

John was the busheller and it was the most unpleasant of jobs because pickers were always arguing that you were putting too much in the bushel, then they would have a strike because they weren't earning enough money. If he got some good pickers and they would clean it of leaves, he would bushel light. But if he got someone who wouldn't clean the leaves from the hops, the elbow went in – but not noticeably – and he would bushel heavy. I can remember one or two not happy with him and they would say, "you're bushelling heavy!" And all he would say was, "no, I'm just bushelling normal."

Bushellers were no strangers to aggrieved pickers, but some got the better of them, Monica Symonds for instance:

I was picking at Hancock's once at Bishops Frome and Mr Hancock said, "Monica, your hops are too dirty!" And I said, "Mr Hancock you can please yourself if you take them or not". So, he took them. We didn't want them pushing their elbow in, didn't like that. We knew all the bushellers, Arthur Gough and Mr Mitton, and the girls who used to do the booking, Audrey Bullivant and her sister Denise. I think they came from London. We all got on really, they knew what I was like!

Some of the best growers in the region tried their hand at bushelling too. When Graham Andrews returned to the family farm after leaving college in the late 1940s, his father promoted him to head busheller. It didn't take long, however, for Graham to learn that the pay of £1 per week, with regular verbal attacks as the only bonus, was not what he planned for, and started looking for a hop farm of his own.

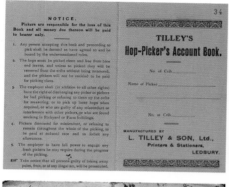
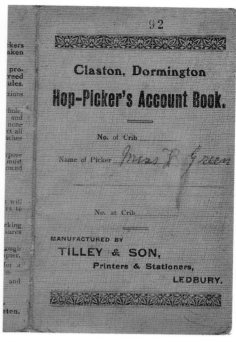

Hop pickers' account books, including for Claston, Dormington (© Peter Green)

Frank Nicklin's mother was from Dudley, and was a veteran of hop picking, knowing all the tricks of the trade when the busheller announced his arrival in the hopyard:

> While the busheller, Mr Mason, was taking the hops from another crib nearby, Mother would immediately lean over and, with both arms covered in hops, would lift them to aerate them. She would say, "them hops are lying solid on the bottom and if you don't lift them up the bushel man can get more hops in his basket and that means less money for us". Mother was very crafty.

While the busheller took the abuse, and often gave it back, the booker was quietly marking down the numbers in a notebook. After a long day in the yard, the booker tallied up how much money was earned by each numbered crib and this was paid out at the end of the harvest. A booker at Ashperton worked long days at George Harrington's Mill End Farm in the 1940s:

A busheller and bagger at work in a Dormington hopyard (© Derek Foxton)

In the 1940s the price per bushel was around 1/2d to 1/3d. The pickers
had to pick all day and every day to make any money, and their fingers
were all black and sticky, while they lived in primitive conditions. After
a long day, the booker then tallied up how much money was earned by
each numbered crib. On the way back to their barracks they used to pick
mushrooms and I used to sell them milk and eggs.

Some pickers learned quickly that keeping the busheller and the pole pullers
on your side was beneficial. Lee McColgan gives an account of picking hops
at Ivington with his aunt in the 1950s:

We would quickly find our crib and compete in shouting for the farm
labourers to come and cut down some of the bines which towered over
us, then away we would go, scratting the hops off the bines and getting
scratched doing it. We tried to keep as many leaves out of the crib as
possible. Not only were we dependent on the labourers for supplying us

with bines, but also dependent on them for moving the crib for us when we had finished cropping, so we kept them sweet with drinks or fags.

But if we upset them, they would refuse to collect our hops at the end of the day unless we cleansed our crib of leaves, which would make everyone late for getting home. The whole day my auntie would go on like this, standing at the crib, stripping the hops off the bines, only stopping and waiting for more bines or to be moved, or for refreshments. I can see her now, dressed in an apron, with a turban on her head, woodbine in her mouth, and her hands darting back and forth as she picked the hops.

Rather like getting your towel on the sunbed at the pool before everyone else, there was a race to get the best crib in the hopyard. Hops growing on the edges were not considered the best place to pick. Good-sized hops were generally found in the middle of the yard. Alec Haines was sent off on his bike very early each morning, his prime objective to get the best-placed crib: 'I used to leave at 4am every day to the hopyard for my mother, to get a good crib and a nice place. I had four jars with four candles in until it became light. I'd be picking and then the rest of the family would turn up.'

As with the hop kiln, the work of the busheller seems to have been a male-only occupation. However, not so at Deans Place, Yatton, near Ross-on-Wye. Three generations of Cottons grew hops here, bussing in pickers from nearby Ross-on-Wye, Tudorville and Brampton Abbots. Peter Cotton's maiden aunt showed him the ropes:

When I eventually came home from school, one of my first jobs was to do bushelling. My father's maiden sister, Dorothy or Dorrie, lived with us. She used to bushel the hops until I took it over in 1951 or 1952 and I suppose I learnt it off her. She was a formidable lady. She was able to put up with the back chat, and there was often a bit of that. As long as you were consistent the pickers didn't mind. They used to strike now and again and then they wouldn't pick and you had to negotiate with them. The Hide at Woolhope, that was their firing point: "oh, they're paying this and that there". But there was never any great animosity.

Hop Tokens and Tally-Sticks

Prior to the use of account books after the Second World War, hop tallies and hop tokens were used to keep track of how many hops had been picked by each picker, and thus what each would earn on pay day.

TALLY-STICKS

A tally-stick is a piece of wood, typically around 15 inches long, which was split lengthways. For each bushel or basket of hops, a mark would be filed across the two halves of the tally-stick, with one half retained by the picker and the other by the tally-man. As only two halves would marry up perfectly, it was a simple and effective way of ensuring that both the picker and the tally-man had an accurate record of what had been picked. At the end of the picking, the two halves of the tally-stick would be reunited, and payment worked out on the basis of the number of grooves, and thus of bushels or baskets picked.

A tally-man scoring his tally-sticks in a hopyard at Newton Dilwyn, 1903
(posed photograph by Alfred Watkins © Hereford Libraries)

HOP TOKENS

Hop tokens were a coin-like form of currency used on hop farms from c.1780 until the 1940s. They were 'minted' in a variety of sizes and materials, including brass, iron, zinc and lead, and range from the crude and simple to the beautiful and elaborate. Typically, each token would have a number on one side (for the number of baskets or bushels, or cash equivalent) and the grower's name or initials on the other side. In the same way as tallies, they could be handed out in the hopyard and cashed in on pay day.

Herefordshire hop token in pewter, probably nineteenth-century and thought to be for a farmer called Richard Knight
(© R. Wheeler)

Kentish sixpence hop token in brass, dated 1767, for John Toke of Godington near Ashford. *Note bushel of hops with 'no pains no gains' above*
(© Baldwin's of St James)

East Sussex hop token in pewter, probably nineteenth-century, for Robert Eldridge, Norton's Farm, Sedlescombe
(© Baldwin's of St James)

East Sussex hop token in pewter, dated 1845, for Edward Lord, tenant of Goteley Manor, Northiam
(© Baldwin's of St James)

PAYDAY AND A BIT OF STRIKING

In my father's time there were strikes during the hand-picking days. So, he got the buckets out and gave them plenty of cider and next morning they were back at work! It always happened like that. **Simon Parker, Instone Court, Munderfield**

There was pay and then there was striking. Some growers came to expect it and started off at a lower rate. Tom Nellist's grandfather, William, at Horsham Farm, Martley, knew it was as much a part of harvest time as cribbing was:

> First thing they would do is have a couple of days of hop picking then they would go on strike for more money. Then the other local growers would get together and decide what they were going to pay them. It always happened like that.

Worries over the Second World War didn't stop pickers demanding more money. A beleaguered Mr H.J. Davies of Paunceford Court had to put up with a strike for several days, while his precious crop languished, only for his pickers to return to work at the same rates of pay! There were similar shenanigans in 1957 at Hill End Farm, Weston Beggard when 30 strikers walked out for five days. The pickers, mostly from Ebbw Vale, demanded 11d a bushel instead of the 10½d offered. Farmer Mr Godson refused their demand. In a show of support, another 50 pickers dropped tools and stopped working on the picking machine. They had met their match: Mr Godson stood his ground, and they all returned to work having won no increase in pay.

The arrival of a different type of striker from the Dudley and Walsall aircraft component works raised concerns in a yard at Bromyard in 1939. The workers had dropped tools at their West Midlands base and staged a walkout. Eager to keep money coming in, they came where there was an endless supply of work: the hopyards. They were not particularly welcomed, however. The *Hereford Times* reported: 'It was hoped they would not have an unsettling influence on the pickers, for strikes were not unknown!'

Violet Eastham and other disgruntled pickers went on strike until there was a change in bushelling habits:

> You'd be lucky if the busheller got three bushels out of a crib-full. But one year he only measured us two. So, when he came round I said, "do

you want any help to fill that basket up – you've no need to put your bloody elbow in as well as your feet." So, we went on strike and made cups of tea and something to eat. Eventually he came and said, "Aren't you going to pick?" "We'll pick," I said, "when you alters your tune!"

Earnings from hop picking were crucial and hard-hit families used their earnings to buy winter coats, shoes, fuel, food and even, in one case, a tin bath. However, others spent theirs in novel, non-essential ways. Hereford sprinter Madeline Haines went hop picking to pay for her tracksuit and spiked running shoes. 'I bought a hand-made pair, from Jennings Sports in Eign Gate', she said. Another spent her earnings on 'Dinky curlers which cost 8/4d. I thought I was the cat's whiskers with my new-found curls!' And in 1944, the farm foreman at E.B. & D.H. Thompson at Ledbury, enjoyed a new pair of Wellington boots thanks to the hop-picking efforts of his wife and daughter.

A family hand-picking together in a Bromyard hopyard (© John Symonds)

Saving souls in the hopyards was a serious business for Missionaries. For many pickers it provided some welcome entertainment, and probably hope too. William Luff of the Plymouth Brethren was dedicated to his missionary work in the West Midlands hopyards in the early 1900s. He was no slouch when it came to spreading his message. In a typical month in Herefordshire and Worcestershire, he walked 300 miles, visited 188 hopyards and preached and distributed the gospel to over 14,000 adults, beside twice as many children. This was a man who used every opportunity to spread the faith, despite the challenges of his audience, including this one at Frith Common:

> One party of 500 were very rough men and woman using dreadful language. In most hopyards, we stand in the centre of the people at their work and sing a gospel hymn. In one last year, the farmer was bushelling his hops, a rather unfavourable time for us; but the people specially asked, "Will you sing us the hymn you sang last year?" We began it, and the master kindly stopped bushelling until we had finished the song, and also a brief exhortation, listening and thanking us for what we had done. The way we are received by the owners is most encouraging.

Missionaries and children holding up Mission newspapers in a hopyard near Ross-on-Wye
(© *Ross Gazette*)

One woman had four of our Almanacs from previous years decorating the walls of her house, another wanted one in memory of her son who was at the war. The war is a grim reality to these poor people, who have given their best to protect our land. We scarcely went to a crib where the pickers had not someone fighting, wounded or killed; and again and again the pickers said, "I shall send this to France," or elsewhere. One man picking said, "The Germans have given me a kiss since I last saw you", and pointed to wounds in both cheeks, where a bullet had gone right through, causing partial lock-jaw. We had a straight talk with him. Another was in the hopyard whose fingers had been shot away. The word was preached to the pickers at their work, and many of them have carefully taken to their homes the messages received.

A charity crib at Ankerdine (© Peter Walker)

Children were expected to pull their weight too and pick their quota before play-time. Dolly Thomas of Ledbury was one of them, but she had an incentive:

If you didn't get your hops picked then you had nothing to put on your card and then no money. And that meant you didn't go to the Hop Fair because it came after the picking in October. So, you picked your hops to pay for a ride at the fair.

Children picking hops at Dormington (*above* © Tony Williams, Derek Foxton Archive; *left* © Miss White), and at Withington in 1968 (*below* © Derek Evans/ HARC). *Bottom*: an extract from the hop-picking diary for Knightwick (© Peter Walker)

Church Army Captain Hotchkiss stayed at the Manor + worked in the neighbourhood. Lantern lectures, concertina + singing + services.

There were other entertainments in the hopyards, including magic lantern shows, film shows and singing. In the 1950 season, two Birmingham boys found entertainment on the famous Shelsey Walsh hill climb motor-racing event. They were hop picking in the Teme Valley with their families and were drawn to the sounds of motor cars climbing the famous track:

> They were training, and we went to watch from one of the steep embankments. It was free and a schoolboy's dream. On one of our walks through the woods, we found ourselves on very soft ground. We decided to investigate and clawed away at the soft covering. About a foot down we came upon a treasure, hundreds of unsold hill climb programmes buried there in perfect condition. For two destitute Brummie back-street kids, this was treasure indeed. Kids that couldn't even afford a comic book, now had real books to read. I can still smell the printer's ink that rose to meet us out of that buried treasure.

Another source of entertainment in the hopyards was 'cribbing'. At the end of the season, and mostly in jest, men and boys pushed girls and women into cribs, grabbing a kiss, and then it was the turn of the women and girls to chase the men and boys into the crib. Other times the aim was to push the busheller in. It's remembered fondly as flirtatious fun, but it could get out of hand. In October 1915 a hop picker, a collier from Ebbw Vale, was charged with assault after cribbing a 14-year-old girl, also from Ebbw Vale, at Showle Court, Yarkhill. 'It's no good me cribbing you if I don't kiss you', he was heard to say. The Chairman of the Bench declared, 'if the prisoner had known the girl was the tender age she was, he would not have attempted to crib her'. He was jailed for a month.

'Cribbing', Stanford Bridge (© Robert Jones)

Mrs Edith Young, seated second from left, was the 'ganger' from the Putson area of Hereford. She recruited these pickers, and others, for picking at Claston, Dormington. Her daughter, Margaret Wheatstone, sits on the crib far right (© Wheatstone Family/ HARC)

TIME FOR SOME BAIT

When we were in the hopyard, we used to get a stick, a certain type of stick it was. Dad used to skin it and then he pushed it through the bacon and cooked it over the fire and held the bread, and then let the fat drip on the bread. I've never tasted anything like it since and I doubt I ever will. Ray Fisher, 'Reminiscences of Leominster Life Project', Leominster Museum

Images of stews bubbling in cast iron pots over golden braziers, leave the viewer salivating. Smells and tastes are evocative and very much part of the collective memory. Pliny, the Roman author, wrote of young hop shoots being used as vegetables, a poor man's asparagus. Meanwhile, John Gerard, in his 1597 *Herball*, described hop asparagus as 'more toothsome than nourishing'. Either way, it was a vegetable still being enjoyed by a Bishops Frome postman in the 1960s, who was known to snip young shoots off while on his delivery rounds, to be fried with butter later in the day.

Left: Ben Green (*left*) and his cousin Bill Went (*right*) having tea at Pomona (© Peter Green)
Right: Tea time at The Vauld, Marden (© June Gwynne)

Don Davies worked with hops for Mr Powell at Hall Court, Rushall, as a young man, but as a child he walked from Gorsley with his mother, younger brother and two sisters, to pick at Cottons of Upton Bishop. Quite a walk for youngsters, but his mother had, like so many like her, the pram: 'She used to bring the old pram with us and in it she would put her own kettle and tea pot, sandwiches and cake and maybe a child or two. At tea-time Mum would make a fire. Hops got into everything; I can still smell them now.'

Peter Cale worked for Bruff picking machine engineers, but as a lad he enjoyed evenings sitting around a camp-fire at his grandfather's hop farm, Batchcombe, Suckley:

> It was an area with a hearth and open fire and they always had a stew in a big pot. While they were in the yard it would be simmering away all day and in the evening we all sat around it on tree trunks and logs eating the stew. There would probably be a bit of rabbit in it and swedes off the farm. Tasted good though.

An iron-framed contraption, the 'devil' was the focus of cooking operations in barracks. The farmer provided the coke (the kiln would be hungry for that too), and above the glowing embers, blackened pots and kettles of all shapes and sizes, hung from hooks over the fire, strong tea always on the go.

Hop pickers take a tea break at Dormington (© Derek Evans/ HARC)

In the hopyards, pickers built small fires for break-time tea, or, if they were lucky, the farmer's wife would pour tea brought to the yard on the back of a horse-drawn cart. For the more sophisticated, it was the Primus stove. John Ridgeway, 83, had the responsibility of lighting theirs:

> At 11.30 we were allowed to light the methylated spirit stove and put on the kettle. When it boiled we stopped for dinner, which was an assortment of sandwiches, cheese, pickle, tomatoes, or meat, and best of all, egg and bacon pie, which Mum made each evening. That was always followed by slabs of home-made fruit cake, tea and orange squash. When we finished, and everything packed away, we were allowed to play and explore the woods, in the streams, make pipes with grass tobacco and try to smoke them, or go into the orchard and pinch apples!

It was a happy time for one grower's daughter at Acton Beauchamp:

> We kept the milk and eggs, and other bits and pieces, and the pickers
> would come to the house and buy whatever they needed. On Sundays,
> the women came in and peeled a large sack full of potatoes which were
> cooked in the furnace, and we roasted a huge joint of beef – I had never
> seen one so big – and after the gravy had been put on the plates, it
> was my job to carry them out to the wall in the courtyard, and all the
> pickers came and collected their lunch. There was one Cockney chappie
> who always stopped at the village shop on his way to buy me a box of
> chocolate. The last I heard of him he was in jail.

The two world wars did not interrupt hop picking, and pickers still required
accommodation and food. It was complicated somewhat by the food ration-
ing system. But there were ways around this, remembers Ray Morris:

> In the war-time when they came out of the towns, there was rationing.
> If they tried to go to the butchers in Tenbury, he had their coupons for
> meat, but he put their meat under the counter for the black market and
> they couldn't get much food. So Mother used to always make sure she
> had plenty of boiling fowls, old hens that had gone past laying. She
> never got rid of them because she knew they would need them in the hop
> picking. The hop drier used to put rabbit snares down and night lines
> down in the river for eel. Used to keep everyone going.

Over at Ankerdine, Peter Walker's mother, Sheila, was heavily involved in
hop operations, managing the food-rationing situation with military precision and ingenuity:

> Rationing came in during hop picking, so all the pickers we had in 1941/
> 1942 were registered at the Knightwick post office, so all their ration
> cards were Knightwick ones. She'd have to buy in a big box of butter and
> cut it up into half-ounce pieces and dish it out to each family, and she
> would buy from the wholesaler in Worcester and wash the maggots off
> the bacon and that sort of thing before giving it out to them. One or more
> hairy stories.

In October 1927, *The Dudley Chronicle*, described the 'penny meal', a cheap way of feeding a group of pickers:

> Two nights each week, we are given potatoes. A certain quantity is given to each picker. These help make many good meals. We were a party of eight, and I peeled all eight potatoes, then I went down to the shop for a large-sized onion and some tinned meat and an Oxo. Then I boiled it all in the pot on the huge fire. It was really very nice. To think that eight persons had partaken of a substantial feast for the small sum of one penny each.

Fish-seller to the hopyards, Mrs Hannah Brace from Ledbury, displayed a no-nonsense, slap-the-fish-on-the-counter, buy-it-if-you-want-it approach to customer service. She was without ceremony, was known to wash fish in brooks on arrival at the hopyards and once slapped a kipper back on the slab after it had been grabbed by a farm dog. Both she and her customers were unperturbed – and, as far as can be established, unharmed. Gladys Barnett called her the fish lady:

Fish-seller Mrs Brace, selling her wares in Ledbury. Her daughter, Hannah, also went on to become a fish-seller around the hop-growing district (© Richard Brace)

She used to come around at hop picking in a pony and trap and bring fish, kippers, tomatoes and lardy cakes. My Mum said one day, "I've brought no money down today". But Mrs Brace would give her some tomatoes for our lunch and say, "you can pay me on Saturday". And there was no fear you weren't going to pay because she had a stall under the market house in Ledbury, where the bus used to load up. You couldn't have got on the bus without her seeing you, so she was always sure of her money. And if you hadn't been to her, she would come to the bus stop and shout, "where's your money, Mrs?"

Margery Hunt had the unusual privilege of tasting something you hear about only in folklore while she was hop picking:

> There was a Gypsy man picking for us named Malpiard. We had a fire going and he said, "can I use your fire?" Because he wanted to roast a hedgehog. So he put it in, in its skin, then when it was done he got him out of the ashes and just skinned it and it was nothing but a lump, like a chicken's breast. And I said, "you're not going to eat that are you?" And he said, "I am, it's all I've got today". And it was beautiful. He said that his family practically lived on them when they didn't have much food.

Ice cream was a popular sight in the hopyard, as were the other local shop keepers, grocers, bakers and butchers, who went mobile to reach their captive audiences across the hop-growing areas. 'I used to accompany my father, who was a baker, into the hop fields each day with large four-pound batch loaves and the ever popular, 'Lemster bread pudding', which my father made trayfuls of every day during the hop season.'

A queue forming with arrival of the ice-cream seller in a hopyard (© Brian Willder)

Selling goods in the hopyard: Joan Perry and father Bert, from Worcester (© Martin Staines)

Visiting bakers and butchers created great opportunities for farm dogs. Sheila Pinches recalls one particular incident at Hancocks of Wyercroft, Bishops Frome: 'The local baker and butcher used to visit the barracks to sell the pickers bread and meat. One time the farm dog got in the back of the van and had a wonderful time!'

Tom Nellist's grandmother, Annie, ran a farmhouse shop like many farm-wives (hers was in Horsham) for the duration of the picking season, providing basic needs, such as bread, butter, milk, flour, sugar and salt. But there were treats in store for the pickers, said Tom: 'The fish and chip van would come in the evenings and a travelling wholesaler would come on a Friday or Saturday. I well remember the ladies asking for steak, which up 'til then I thought was something that held a fence up!'

Janet Pearce's (née Stubbs) mother ran a shop for three farms at Canon Frome – Southfield, White House and Hansnett:

My eldest brother, Ron, was fascinated by the Gypsies and their way of life and went to live with them during one hop picking and we were told not to acknowledge him if we saw him riding past on a dray. There were two big Gypsy families at Southfield: the Stevens and the Loveridges. Bill Loveridge would give Father a wad of money at the beginning of hop picking to keep for him, and at the end of the season all the Gypsies settled up their shop bills with Mother. But Father hated the season, because he spent long hours day and night on lookout for poachers.

Helme, J., *Hops'n'Hoptons, a History of Canon Frome, Herefordshire*, 2001

Some growers took scrumping for apples or digging up potatoes or marrows in their stride. Others took it far more seriously. Tales of pickers arriving with light luggage and leaving with boxes that had to be dragged and hoisted onto waiting lorries, were commonplace. Mr Paske of Bromyard came up with a generous solution. On the last day of picking he allowed workers to help themselves to apples. Pickers at Ellen Partridge's went home laden with pears, apples, potatoes, damsons and nuts. Alas, one farmworker who was very proud of marrows he had carefully tended on a muck tump, was never to taste them. On the day the pickers left, he found they had all been lifted out.

Some did suffer the consequences though. In October 1935, Lily Swift and Rosa Sage, married women of Pengan, Glamorgan, Arthur Jones unemployed of Pengan, and Thomas Price unemployed of Abergargoed, were charged with the theft of potatoes from a field belonging to Philip Davies of Claston, Dormington. The defendants were fined 7s. 6d. The Chairman said: 'These troubles always occur about hop-picking time and are caused by hop pickers who have no respect for property'. And in September 1940, two youths, Alfred Smith and Harry Butler, 'hop pickers of no fixed abode, pleaded guilty to trespass in pursuit of conies at Birchend Farm, on the Canon Frome Estate. The youths were found in a coppice with rabbits, ferret and nets, by the hop dryer, Mr Morris. Each defendant was ordered to pay costs'.

John Pudge of Frogend acted swiftly, recalls son Charles, after pickers tried scrumping. He might have been hard-of-hearing, but he didn't miss a trick:

My father was deaf. He had been in the First World War with a machine gun, but he could still pick up dull thuds, so he could hear them shaking the apples. He'd sort of walk half-way across the orchard, and I can remember he had a particularly vicious collie, and he used to send it after them and once they started to run, the dog would be biting them. Father used to stand there laughing.

Margaret Wheatstone's mother, Edith, had a close shave at Claston. A neighbouring and disgruntled farmer complained that the apples from his orchard were being scrumped and he was going to search the buses: 'Luckily, he didn't search Mum's and a good job too because underneath her seat were a box of pears and a box of apples! Dad wrapped them in newspaper and they were lovely for Christmas.'

Evacuated children from Birmingham and Liverpool are taking the place of imported pickers in Herefordshire and Worcestershire hopyards, and they are throwing themselves into the work with vigour and enthusiasm. Hereford Times, September 1942

War-time wrought changes in the hopyards of the West Midlands. With men away in the forces and many women joining the war effort and working in munitions or other associated industries, the profile of the picker changed. Headscarf and apron wearers still came, but in reduced numbers. Joining the picking ranks were the Land Army girls, evacuees, prisoners-of-war (POWs) and, intriguingly, a test pilot. In 1943 Michael Daunt (1909–91) was at the controls of the British and Allied jet fighter, the Gloster Meteor. It was the first British combat aircraft to be powered by Frank Whittle's revolutionary invention, the jet engine. A hop picker interviewed in the 1980s, remembers him working in a hopyard at Castle Frome, 'suffering from stress'. She was thrilled when Daunt returned to his day job after his recuperation and kept his promise, when he flew low over the farm at 4pm and looped the loop!

Across the county at Moreton Camp, schoolboy Philip Price remembered American GIs commandeering the kilns. Not to cook hops though: 'They weren't in use then. It was where they used to store corn beef!' Like the rest of the country, black-out rules applied and, in the barracks, after a long day in the yards, there was a great sorting out of old clothes and brown paper to stop light escaping through chinks in the walls and windows. Meanwhile, from their hill-top farm at Bishops Frome, the Partridge family watched Coventry burn more than 60 miles away to the east. Janet Parker remembers that evening very well:

> We slept downstairs and our front room was full of gas masks as Dad was the ARP Warden for our area. I do remember being held up and being told, 'that is Coventry on fire!' We also saw searchlights at night picking up the planes that went over and once a barrage balloon broke free of its moorings and dragged a wire behind it, which Dad thought might cut the wires of the hopyard. Fortunately, it missed, but I did get a doll's dress made out of the parachute silk. It was made by a dressmaker, Miss Ethel Southall, from Fromes Hill. I still have that doll.

Left: A prisoner-of-war working as a bagger (© Brian Willder). *Right*: German POWs at Pomona Farm, Bartestree, during the Second World War (© Herefordshire Lore)

Similarly, a young boy in hopyards at Canon Pyon still has a tin car fashioned from a can, made by a German POW.

Tanks hidden among pear tree orchards were spied by Pat Hunt (née Sherlock), who, as a ten-year-old in 1943, visited her great-aunt Maud Willetts, who was picking hops at Leigh Sinton. Maud, and her mother before her, were chain makers from the Cradley Heath area. They were also gangers, making up lists of pickers from Cradley Heath, Netherton and even London. It was just a day trip for Pat, but it was some trip for a girl still at primary school:

> I went with my father, Percy Sherlock, and I was on the back of the tandem. We did a round trip of nearly 65 miles, from Halesowen to Leigh Sinton. The farm was Wendon's, Chirkenhill. We would normally ride out to Hartlebury to pick and buy fruit, but this time we went further because Dad wanted to check on his mother, Granny Sherlock, who had decided to go down to the hopyard one last time to visit her sister, Maud. So we just went for the day and then cycled home again.

Doris Kershaw lives in Worcester today, but during the summer of 1939, she was 13 years old and a pupil of Lord Scudamore Girls School. The hops still had to be picked, however, and school children were enlisted to the ranks of the pickers:

Evacuee children on a
wagon ride at Suckley
(© Muriel Griffiths)

Evacuee children
enjoying a birthday
party at Suckley
(© Muriel Griffiths)

A wonderful school memory was hop picking. Our class travelled
daily by bus to a nearby farm. It was not signposted so sadly I cannot
remember where it was! The hops grew on large poles which men
brought over to huge canvas cribs into which we picked the hops. Twice
a day, bushellers came and measured what we had picked. Every basket
held a bushel of hops. While the teachers went for lunch, we threw one
another into the cribs and I will always remember the wonderful smell
as we landed! Miss Knot, one of the teachers, was stung in the mouth by
a wasp and had to be taken to a doctor immediately, which we thought
very exciting – poor soul!

John Thacker, lived and grew up in Upper Sapey. During the war he was
working at Boswick Farm, Wolferlow, where he met his future wife, a Land
Army Girl:

It was a warm day in 1943 and I was working in the Old Hop yard. Shirley was a Land Army girl scuffling between the rows with the one hoe pulled by Lively, the old cart-horse. At the end of the rows the headland wasn't wide enough, and Shirley kept catching off the last beet in the row. The Boss wasn't best pleased. But when Shirley came around he was all smiles and offered her his tobacco tin. 'I don't want any baccy' she said, but when she opened it she found a gold sovereign. She had scuffled it up on the headland. We've still got that sovereign now, but I often wonder about the poor old hop picker in years gone by who had dropped it. What a loss that must have been for him.

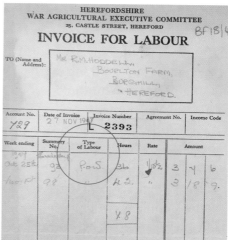

Above: Invoice for POW labour at Bourlton Farm, Burghill (© HARC). *Left*: Land Army girl hop picking at Knightwick in September 1942 (© Peter Walker)

The arrival of Italian and German prisoners-of-war added some interest for curious locals. At Hansnett an Italian prisoner, Guilio, was dropped off every day by lorry. He was well-liked and caught rabbits and birds, eating them with spaghetti to the fascination of onlookers. He also made rings out of 6d and 3d coins. Other POWs were at Baldwin's from the White House, and would drop by and visit Guilio. The Italians made an even bigger impression in another yard near Ledbury, where they sang operatic arias around the crib. It was said swooning hearts was a common ailment at the time.

Sheila Hince's (née Jones) hop-picking efforts during the war were rewarded:

> When I got a bit older I wanted a bicycle. My father, who was in the army, made me a small crib and my mother said I had to pick hops to save the money for it. I was only nine but when the hop picking finished, I had £9. I was so excited I went to Watsons in Commercial Road in Hereford to purchase it. It cost £10 and Mum gave me the extra £1. It was a little too large for me and they had to put wooden blocks on the pedals, so I could reach them and cycled home the eight miles to Burley Gate. The cycle was a 'Victory', prompting Mum to remark, "I hope that the war will soon be over, and we will have victory." Within a year we did!

War-time spirit, all pulling together, has been celebrated in the decades since the end of the war. But some of these mining boys from South Wales were willing to risk prosecution for their 'French leave', and who can blame them. In an attempt to stem the flow of labour to the hopyards, in 1943 collieries across the Valleys put up posters admonishing those who went hop picking:

> While it is felt that all colliery workers must realise the present needs of the country sufficiently well not to give cause for complaint this year in regard to absenteeism for hop picking. It is desirable to make it clear that permission to go hop picking will not be given to any worker employed in a scheduled occupation in the coal mining industry, that it would make it an offence to leave the coal mining industry. Prosecutions must follow absenteeism.

The bombings of London and other major cities must have seemed a long way away, but that changed for John Barnett in the 1940s when a bomb landed in hopyards at Aldersend, Tarrington:

> I was at my granny's and we heard a whistling sound that was coming not far from where my father was working on the wirework. He wasn't allowed to go into the hopyard the next day. When the bomb was dug out it was full of sand. Well, they reckon some of the slave workers made the weight of the bomb right but didn't put any explosives in. It makes you think, doesn't it?

A few days out in the fresh air of a hopyard was considered to be a good antidote for any number of health conditions, according to doctors and medical professionals. A young woman in Staunton-on-Wye, suffering from rumbling appendicitis, was feeling rather depressed being stuck at home. 'Go hop picking', advised her doctor, 'the fresh air will do you good'. He was right. Mrs Julian Gallimore, recovering from whooping cough, received similar advice.

Conversely, there was recognition by local authorities that the congestion of pickers could easily be a breeding ground for all sorts of pests and diseases. Bye-laws made by the Rural District Council of Hereford stipulated that 'any inmate of tents, vans, sheds and similar structures [who] is ill of infectious disease, shall thereupon immediately give notice to the Medical Officer of Health'. The impact of disease could easily be carried back to the industrial centres many of these pickers came from and have grave, epidemiological consequences beyond the benign hopyard. In the pre-First World War period, an outbreak of typhoid in Dudley was the result of an infection being carried directly from the hop-growing districts:

> The recent outbreak in the Borough was attributed to liquid filth
> getting into drinking water, and steps had been taken to prevent the
> introduction of infection into the Hopfields in the first place. And as
> recently as 1939 there were six cases of diphtheria among hop pickers at
> Leigh Sinton and two at Shelsley Beauchamp. Medical Officer Dr Parry
> said the diminished ventilation occasioned by the black-out "had been a
> great problem."

But there were significant improvements by the 1950s, with pickers receiving better healthcare by this period. Such changes received the approval of Mrs Fanny Overton of Shropshire, who had picked (or been present) at Kyrewood Farm, Tenbury, for all of her 56 birthdays. Like her mother and grandmother before her, she was charge-hand and mouthpiece in the yard: 'What with the properly built barracks, field kitchens and daily visits from the district nurse, things have certainly changed for the better. It's always been a good holiday – far better than going to Blackpool.'

Folk medicine was still available to those who sought it in the post-war years. Hereford's Medicine Man, known as Gypsy Lee, was a purveyor of some unusual remedies. Stripped to the waist in all weathers, 'he had the most wonderful sun tan while selling his miracle cures', an onlooker observed. For those afflicted with rheumatism, he recommended the application of hedgehog grease, fat produced by boiling a hedgehog.

Help was available for cuts, stings and bruises from hopyard surgeries, and district nurses administered first aid, arriving in hop-growing areas with medicine bags full of bandages, plasters and calamine lotion. In *Pyon Years,* Lena Southworth recalled her mother holding busy surgeries with help from a friend, a lady doctor from Bath: 'If she could not come, two Missionary nurses would come. On one occasion they delivered a baby in the hop shed and the lady got up the next day and started picking hops again!'

At Bosbury, in 1941, the Hop Pickers Mission commandeered the parish hall for a surgery, 'from 6pm to 8pm, where hundreds of minor cases received first-aid treatment'. But there was little first-aid could do to help some of the pickers. At Canon Frome, the death of a seven-year-old, Eva Fletcher, is still remembered by her Forest-of-Dean descendants. In September 1934, following a fall, Eva from Cannop, Coleford, who was hop picking with her family, became ill. Nurse Theodora Crabtree of the Diocesan Hopfields Mission attended her, but sadly the child died. It wasn't just pests and diseases that caused health problems: shock could too, as Doris Helme experienced. Doris (née Mayo) was born in Swinmore Common in 1913. As a young married woman, she moved to Castle Frome and picked hops for the Paynes:

> I was coming out of the hopyard with a friend and she had her two
> children in the pram and I'd got my bike. Suddenly it started thundering.
> I wasn't scared of thunder until that night. I was pushing my bike with
> one hand and helping her along with the other, and she hadn't rubber
> handles on the pram, it was just bare, and I got hold of it and the
> lightning went right up my arm and my hair stood on end. I've never
> been so scared in my life. The babies in the pram were fine. I can almost
> feel it now. Even now when it thunders, I'm frightened.

When in the 1940s Sam Howards fell between the buffers of the coach and the train at Bromyard Station, there was a cry for help. Howards had just arrived

Clockwise from above left: Pole puller Jim North at Nettlestead Farm, 1958 (© Georgina Wheeler); Bank Farm, 1960s (© David Powell); Tenbury picker (© Roy James); Victorian pickers (© Richard Brace); Ivor Price and Robert Jones, Avenbury Court, 1967 (© John Symonds). *Above*: Cigarette break, Pigeon House Farm, Leigh (© Janet Davis)

at the station from his home in Wolverhampton. He was visiting friends hop picking. Stepping off the train, the young man fell over backwards, between the buffers and onto the rails. He was immediately extricated and taken by wheelbarrow to Dr Lewis, who found the man had sustained a scalp wound and bruises. With great fortitude, Mr Howard blamed no one but himself, before being taken off to the Workhouse, presumably to recuperate.

BIRTHS, DEATHS AND MARRIAGES

The hopyard, like any other community, had its share of births, deaths and marriages. In many respects it was an informal marriage bureau, and is how Pauline Andrews' parents met:

> Mum, Irene Bradley, started to come hop picking around 1945, when she was 14, with her mum and four siblings, from Tipton. It was their annual holiday and they all looked forward to it. It was at this time she first met Dad, Ray Whiting. He was 16 and worked on the farm they visited, Pridewood near Ashperton. They stayed at the old army barracks there and Dad made sure that they were all well looked after, taking them wood for the fire and keeping them supplied with potatoes. Nothing stopped Mum coming hop picking every year. Whatever job she had at the time in Tipton, she would leave it for the hop picking and find another job when she got home. When she was a bit older, in her late teens/ early 20s, she would go hop picking with two friends from Tipton, Alice and Eileen. Mum ended up marrying my Dad, and Alice and Eileen married his two brothers, Charlie and Toby, and all three brothers worked for the Rimmells at Pridewood Farm.

One young Welsh woman was courted by her young man at Westhope. Mrs Baldwin from Cardiff remembers:

> I met my husband hop picking. He used to carry my crib. I courted him up the hopyards and then married him. We had great fun. It was the only sort of holiday I ever had. We had singing and dancing parties. All the Yeomans were good kind farmers and were very fair with their workers.
>
> **Lynne Pugh,** *The Book of Pyon Years*

There was even a marrying stone at the bottom of Fromes Hill, although its matchmaking qualities had more to do with finding work picking hops than picking husbands or wives. Charles Pudge explains:

When I was a whipper-snapper there was a bloody great stone there, must have weighed three or four tons. When people came looking for hop picking one of the questions growers asked was, "how many of you are there?" If it was just the one, the grower would say, "no, we don't give a crib for one person". So, these singletons used to go and sit on the 'marrying stone' and wait to meet another single person also looking for work picking hops. So, they would go together from there as a 'couple', hence it was always referred to as the marrying stone. They would come back and say, "don't worry boss, the wife's turned up!"

Bishops Frome church could have been the venue for Amy Lane's wedding in the 1930s, but fate intervened. Amy was a Gypsy from Middlesex. Before Amy died, her granddaughter, Raine Geoghegan, recorded her life story. It's an extraordinary oral account of a Gypsy caravan coming to the area for the hops. In Amy's own words:

It used to take us three days to travel to Hereford from Middlesex in our caravans for the hop picking in Bishops Frome. Our motto was, 'let's keep moving'. In the hopyard we used to blow the whistle for dinner, put the kettles on. There were four loads of us and we would lay out our pots and kettles, make the fires up on arrival. We could make good money with the hops. Dad was a good picker. Alfie, who I wanted to marry, he was a clean picker, and I was a dirty picker. For six weeks picking it was about £250. We all wore long skirts then. All night you could see the fires from the Gypsy camps. The locals were warned not to mix with us, but we had some fun at the Green Dragon. There was a bath-full of ale outside.

I was courting Alfie at the time. I got up one morning and Dad said, "look here, don't mess about, go to the church. You've got to get married in Bishops Frome". So I got up the Sunday morning and went to see the vicar. I said to him, "Vicar, could you marry me and my young man? We're from London for the hop picking". And he said, "sorry, my dear, I can't marry you, there might be a fight!" So we married in Ashford instead.

Herefordshire hopyard, 1966
(© Derek Evans/ HARC)

It was no hospital bed for Lynn Stevens' birth. Her extended Romany family, the Stevens and the Royles, were hop picking near Ledbury in the late summer of 1957, when Lynn took her first breath of air in her grandparents' Berkeley trailer, parked up for the duration of the harvest. Grandmother Stevens had another claim to fame. Portrait artist and president of the Royal Academy of the Arts, Sir Alfred Munnings painted a young Mrs Stevens in his depictions of the Gypsy community at work in the hopyards in the early part of the twentieth century (*see pp. 18–19*).

Spot the Celebrity Hop Picker

Evelyn Cooper from Whitestone in Hereford remembers a young Shirley Bassey picking at Dormington. Next door at Claston, Peter Davies met a young school boy and future snooker champion Ray Reardon picking with his mother, also from South Wales. And Tom Jones was said to have joined the Welsh contingent before fame claimed him. Across the valley and another young boy, future pop star and actor Adam Faith picked hops at Stoke Lacy. In the 1960s Richard Blair, the son of George Orwell, joined hop pickers in the area.

THE LONG ARM OF THE LAW – HOPYARD BOBBY

The image of the village bobby, cycling around his patch, distinctive hat strapped aloft, notebook in top pocket, truncheon looped around his belt, is a quintessential part of the British rural scene. They knew their patch and the people in them. The deluge of pickers transformed their communities – pubs were furiously busy, there was laughter, singing, mayhem, the odd ruckus, licentiousness and a bit of theft too. Some turned a blind eye; others acted. Police reinforcements were often brought in from the pickers' home districts. Sleepy Bosbury had an extra Welsh-speaking policeman sent up from the mining valleys, and another came from the Black Country.

In the 1950s Mike Wood was posted to Burley Gate as a young policeman to give extra support to PC Carl Andrews, for the rambunctious hop-picking season, a posting known to Herefordshire Constabulary as 'hop duties'. When Andrews fell ill, it was left to Wood to police the beat, that stretched from Preston Wynne to Stoke Lacy. On his bike one evening, he dropped in on the Plough Inn at Stoke Lacy, and landlord Bill Symonds. What an astute and clever policeman he was:

> There were two groups of hop pickers in there and I could sense the tension. There was a large Welsh lady in one group, who had a beautiful singing voice, but she was very annoyed because the other group from Liverpool included an older lady who was very drunk and trying to out-sing her. I went to the Welsh lady and said in a Welsh accent: "you've got a lovely voice my dear. Don't take any note of that drunken old bitch, you carry on singing!" Then I crossed the room and quietly told the Liverpudlian, "don't take any notice of that fat old Welsh woman – you just carry on". That seemed to diffuse the situation.

Gilbert 'Scotty' Bowler of Frome Valley Transport proved a great support to Bishops Frome police, remembers his son, Philip:

> Hereford used to send two policemen out for the hop picking. But they didn't have any cars. The only transport they had was a push bike! Dad had made a truck out of a car at the garage just for a runabout. Often the policeman would run in the yard saying, "can I have the truck! There's a fight up at the Holly Bush." And they took the truck and away they went. Bit quicker than a bike.

Another constable who went down as a bit of a legend in hop areas was PC Fred Harris of Bishops Frome. The strong arm of the law was needed more than ever during the hop harvest, when Bishops Frome became the Wild West of hop-picking country. Some delicate types avoided it altogether in the harvest season. PC Harris knew by name all the Gypsies and pickers from 'abroad'. As pubs spilled over with pickers spending their hard-earned cash, PC Harris, big and burly, was the man for the job. Russell Bunn knew him and saw first-hand his ability to handle a situation when things got rowdy:

> He was a hard man. During the hop picking these Welshies were going to get him and they brought this fella up from Wales that was gonna give 'im a hiding. Harris got to hear about it and he went into the pub in civvy

Edwardian hop pickers at Stoke Edith station, early twentieth century (© Derek Foxton)

clothes one evening and this fella was bragging about what he was going to do, when Harris just hit him! They reckon this Welshie was in his tent for two or three days before he recovered.

PC Harris went on to enjoy many years of enforcing the law in his own inimitable fashion. When he retired, a collection of over £300 was raised by the pickers, an enormous sum when you consider how little they had to begin with. It was a measure of their affection for him.

The introduction of the 1948 Education Act ended years of parents cocking-a-snook at schooling and taking children hop picking. It marked a major shift in the industry and heralded the beginning of mechanisation – there was no turning back. The *Worcester Chronicle* of September 1953 thought so too: 'A sad position exists in Herefordshire and Worcestershire hopyards. One grower who last year employed 500 pickers has this year engaged only 36 and these will spend most of their time feeding vines into new machines instead of picking hops themselves'.

5

The Revolution:
'battleships for shrimping'

It is sad to know that an ancient old custom is dying, but it is cheering to watch a traditional industry arm itself with the techniques of the twentieth century.
Guinness staff magazine, *The Harp*, Christmas 1946

B Y the end of the Second World War the hand-picked hop harvest was being challenged by the creep of mechanisation. By the late 1950s, 70% of hops were machine-picked. There was to be no going back.

It was not just engineering innovation that pushed these changes through. There were socio-economic ones too. A booming industrial employment in the post-war years, better wages, as well as Midlands and Welsh educational authorities stamping down on hop-picking 'holidays', led to a dwindling labour force. Mechanisation could hardly keep pace. As one Malvern grower in the 1940s commented, 'it's a machine or there will be no hops'.

MACHINES OF COMPLEX INGENUITY OR 'BATTLESHIPS FOR SHRIMPING'
Although an American machine was imported in 1922, it was considered not suitable for picking English hop varieties. The real story of the English hop-picking machine lies with West Midlands companies, McConnell Hinds and Bruff, a pair of engineering successes that emerged out of sleepy England.

Many claimed the accolade for introducing the first machine. Guinness's hopyards at Braces Leigh near Malvern purchased a model in 1937, made in Worcester. 'It wasn't perfect', they admitted to a reporter from the *Evesham Standard & West Midland Observer*, 'more like a battleship for shrimping. But it is by no means the worst ever made'. At the same time, Mr Hawkins of Thinghill Court hosted experts from across the region to a demonstration of a 'mammoth hop picking machine'. It was the invention of two young

Malvern engineers, Mr F.W. McConnell and Mr G.A. Hinds. They were creating quite a buzz in hop-growing circles. The reporter correctly predicted the 'huge social changes this would unleash'. The provisional cost for this machine? A hefty £1,950 – a substantial investment (about £100,000 today).

By 1938 hop grower *par excellence* Norman Edwards of Rosemaund, Preston Wynn (later to be Rosemaund Experimental Husbandry Farm) was reported to be one of three growers in the district to have 'these gigantic machines'. It was driven by a Fordson tractor engine, which 'also drives a dynamo for lighting purposes'. A year later it was the turn of Captain James Bomford of Fladbury. Already an innovator, he had installed an electrically-controlled pumping station, providing water under pressure to his arable fields. In 1939, with the Second World War on the horizon, he had a McConnell Hinds machine installed and, during the following season, invited the Birmingham and District Section of the Incorporated Brewers' Guild to see it in action. A certain Mr Charles Faram (after whom Charles Faram & Co. Ltd, hop suppliers in Malvern, is named) was thanked for arranging the visit. Growers, brewers, merchants: they all had a vested interest in this new technology. Interviewed shortly before his death at the age of 90 in the *Journal of English Hops Limited* (November 1986), Bomford added some interesting detail to his decision to go mechanised:

> It was Jim Nott of Kyrewood who persuaded me to change to growing
> new varieties, which well suited picking machines. It was in the 1930s
> that two inventive engineers, Fred McConnell and George Hinds, started
> work on the hop-picking machine and were eventually introduced to one
> another by my cousin, Douglas Bomford. This resulted in McConnell
> Hinds Ltd, which so revolutionised the picking of hops.

MCCONNELL HINDS

In the 1940s, when Albert Brookes was recovering from TB, he designed the Bruff hop-picking machine. He studied a McConnell Hinds model at a farm up the road from the factory and designed one that outshone it. Bruff dominated after that. Lawrence Lloyd, former Bruff draughtsman

During the Second World War, Bruff stole the march in the hop-picking machine market, leaving pre-war innovator, McConnell Hinds, snapping at its heels. It never recovered and Bruff went on to dominate. Cherry Hinds is

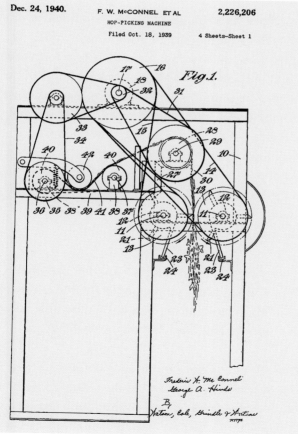

Above: Hinds delivery truck, with Derek Badham, second from left, sitting on the bonnet of the truck (© Derek Badham)

Left: US Patent drawing for a McConnell hop-picking machine, December 1940 (US2226206A)

the daughter of George Hinds, who, together with Freddy McConnell, engineered the first hop-picking machines in the region. Cherry was her father's protégé and eventually worked alongside him from their Barnards Green workshops. She has since gone on to win world-wide plaudits for her model engineering skills. For the last 40 years she has divided her life between Malvern and the States, but after the death of her American husband, she returned to a quiet life here in England.

She is an interesting figure in the story of the picking revolution, although she resolutely refutes that. While women in the post-war years marched to equal rights, equal pay and equal opportunities, she was quietly carving her own career in the male-dominated agricultural machinery field of the 1950s/ '60s/ '70s. Cherry is unimpressed with such epithets, 'it was just a job, for heaven's sake.' Now 89, she recalls McConnell Hinds' early successes:

> My father was from Malvern and Freddy McConnell from Martley.
> They identified the need for a picking machine in the early 1930s. As
> McConnell Hinds, they made the first three at Worcester before the War,
> and moved one to Captain Bomford's of Fladbury, another to Ernest
> Godson in Hereford, and the third to Fred Coleman at Smugley Farm
> in Kent. In 1953 the Smugley machine from Smugley was moved and
> installed by George Hinds Ltd at Edward Lane's at Bosbury Court.
> These machines were known as the 'plucker/ picker bank' because of the
> design of their banks of picking combs, followed by flying fringes, which
> completely stripped the bines. When I was about seven my father took me
> to see a machine at work. It was terribly noisy and truly terrifying – so
> much so I have never forgotten it.

At the outset of War, the Government requisitioned the McConnell Hinds' workshop and production was closed down completely. Mr Hinds switched to working on radar at Malvern College, and Bruff was able to continue uninterrupted and McConnell Hinds was left behind. Cherry:

> After the war, McConnell Hinds came to life again with the Flying
> Finger machine built by another company, but the machines were never
> popular. I remember Father coming back very annoyed because they
> were just not doing things right. By 1964, McConnell Hinds had gone

Cherry Hinds with a couple of her exquisite models

their separate ways and George Hinds Ltd built a prototype Rotobank machine, built with larger hop growers in mind. It was installed at Mr Webb's hop farm at Benchley in Kent. This proved a success and 26 were built at Malvern for the following season, 13 installed in Kent and 13 in Herefordshire and Worcestershire. One even went to Germany and we sold a large static one to a grower/ brewery in Perth, Australia. We also built a mobile Rotobank, and towed it to Germany and demonstrated it there for three weeks. Meanwhile, Bruff went rattling ahead overtaking everything and by 1966 the market had reached saturation point.

McConnell found favour with smaller growers who had lower acreages, and, importantly, were able to customise their machines to existing buildings. Bruff models were much bigger and required new buildings to house them. It was Cherry who was often seen on farms looking at the available space and designing a machine to fit it. At Millend, Castle Frome, they had the space, but lacked the electricity. George Hopkins recalls that first machine:

We had the first hop machine before we even got electricity. But we had a generator and you almost needed two people to turn the handle to get it going. It was like that for about three years then they put the mains electric in. Damn hard work I can tell you. But it changed it a lot. It was a McConnell Hinds machine. Bruff were probably bigger but you had to have a building to put them in. Well,

George Hopkins with a lorry of green sacks at Millend (© George and Lil Hopkins)

a lot of tenant farmers couldn't afford that sort of thing. So, Miss Hinds would come along and say, 'where do you want it?' And she would make it to fit that building. They would build a section and put it on a horse trailer and bring it and fit it in. So simple. It was a far simpler machine than the Bruff and per job I would say it was better. Bruff was bigger and could do more work but took more running and it needed more attention all the time.

Peter Cotton's father had their brand new McConnell Hinds picking machine installed at Deans Place, Yatton near Ross-on-Wye, in 1959:

We had no electricity then of course. That came a few years later, so it ran on a generator until then. I remember Cherry came over with her father quite often. She used to drive a Jenson, a top of the range, big fast car. She was a magic engineer.

Another McConnell Hinds customer was David Powell and his father, of Bank Farm, Rochford. They bought their new machine in 1959 and Cherry again advised them on the model. But father and son did their research first, visiting a lot of growers who had already installed a machine: 'The Bruff was the main one, but what we liked about the Hinds was that it had 13 separate motors on it, mostly direct-driven. The Bruff had three motors so it had a lot of chains and sprockets. Hinds was the best engineering job.'

In the mid-1930s, Albert Brookes opened his Bruff engineering business (so named after his first wife, Barbara Bruff) in the Worcestershire village of Suckley. Electricity had yet to reach the village and in the early days power came from an old car engine set up on a wooden frame; lighting from paraffin lamps hung from the ceiling. By 1945 the first prototype of the Bruff hop-picking machine had been installed at Captain Hutton's at Winthill, not far from Bruffs. From this quiet corner of England, the Bruff was to have a global reach, their machines exported worldwide. There was always going to be a limited capacity for picking machines and by 1978, when CWF Ltd of Ledbury took on the manufacturing of the hop side of Bruff operations, the market was over-subscribed and there were fewer home-based growers.

Lawrence Lloyd, 82, was born in Staffordshire, but returned to live in his father's home village of Suckley in 1949. He began his apprenticeship at Bruff aged 17, starting as a tea boy then working his way up to the drawing office under his boss, Mr Brookes. In 1967, Lawrence went with Brookes to a town near Munich to visit Bruff's West German manufacturer, Scheibenbogen, which had obtained the license to make a mini-Bruff in Germany, suited to German farms with their smaller acreages of hops. Lawrence:

The German company was named after Josef Scheibenbogen and he had his own factory. He came to Bruff at Suckley, once bringing his son with him. There were rumours about what he did in Germany during the war! But I do remember that on his visit there were problems when he arrived because we struggled with translation and also converting measurements from imperial to metric!

On another occasion, Mr Brookes and I went to Czechoslovakia because they wanted fitters and spares from Bruff. Near Prague was a spa town and I remember at the top of the Presidential steps there was still a photo of Hitler! But we were treated like kings and chauffeured out to the hop-fields to see the machines. We were selling machines to them before they started making their own. In the 1970s me and a colleague, Henry Merrick, who was a fitter, had to drive through East Germany on our way to Poland to install three machines there. They would arrive in sections and had to be put together on the farm. Henry had been all over the world with Bruff to Russia, America, Argentina. They were interesting times.

An early Bruff picking machine being trialled in a hopyard. Bruff engineer and designer Albert Brookes is standing on the left (© Brian Willder)

Above left: Bruff name-plate on a Bruff picking machine (© M. O'Mahony)

Above: New Bruff picking machines being delivered by Griffiths Transport of Suckley (© John Griffiths)

BRUFF HOP PICKING MACHINERY

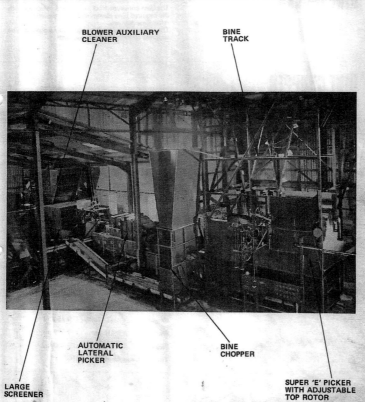

BLOWER AUXILIARY CLEANER

BINE TRACK

AUTOMATIC LATERAL PICKER

BINE CHOPPER

LARGE SCREENER

SUPER 'E' PICKER WITH ADJUSTABLE TOP ROTOR

Left: A page from the Bruff Hop Picking Machinery catalogue, showing the principal parts of a Bruff Super 'E' picker (© Will Kirby, Brook House Hops)

The Bruff has been variously described as '1950s technology at its best' and 'one giant Meccano set'. Both statements are arguably true. There is often a love/ hate relationship with these huge, complex, noisy pieces of machinery. But Brian Willder, manager at Leighton Court, loved them:

> Oh I used to dream about the Bruff. When I went to Hampshire to work on my first hop farm, my main responsibility was looking after the hop machine. I thought it was out of this world. The size of it. I was very keen on Meccano as a boy and a Bruff hop picking machine is just like Meccano.

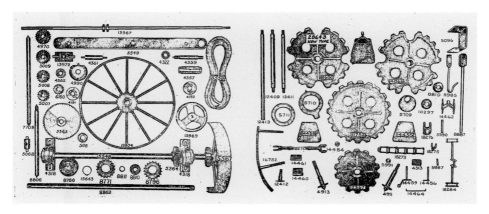

Numbered parts illustrated in the Bruff catalogue (© Will Kirby, Brook House Hops)

The Probert family at Church House Farm, Weston Beggard, purchased an early Bruff model in 1955, and it became a source of curiosity for those who were yet to take the plunge. Tom Probert:

> My Granddad, James Probert, bought it. My dad, John, was relieved because, at 15-years-old, he could see it was a matter of time before he became a busheller and he didn't want that. He remembered quite a few visitors coming out to look at the Bruff when we first got it, just running their eyes over it. When it first came here, Mr Brookes visited to check on it and asked how it was going and Dad said, "well this was wrong, and that was wrong, this bit didn't work". Mr Brookes took it all in then asked, "Was there anything right with it?"

The lack of electricity posed problems for growers eager to move with the times and install a machine. Many villages remained without mains power into the early-1960s. It was a close call for Edward Lewis' family at Upper Eggleton. Their Bruff arrived in 1957, but the power had not! Edward:

> In 1956 we had told the pickers that we wouldn't be wanting them the next year because we knew we would be getting a machine. I think about ten days before picking was supposed to start, the mains electricity poles hadn't even been put in, so we didn't have any electricity supply at all. Eventually they came and put them in, but they had a good bollocking to get them up! It was a bit close, especially as we had cancelled the pickers.

The arrival of this new machine inspired a mix of horror and wonder. But there was an excitement to it too. The arrival of a new Bruff at Carwardine Farm, Lulham was recalled by John Griffiths, then just out of his teens:

> I remember when the Bruff came to Frank Powell's farm in the late 1950s. He said, "we're getting a hop-picking machine", and we all thought, "you can't get a machine to pick hops!" We thought it was a mad idea. But it did, and I ran and looked after it, just picked it up, no one taught me. The problem came if it broke down and you were desperate to get it repaired because you needed the hops for the kiln to dry. If you wanted a part, you just rang Bruff in those days.

Bruff had some big customers including Guinness, Allied Breweries, Clift's at Knightwick and Peter Davies at Claston, who was a frequent visitor to the works and a great friend of Albert Brookes, the Bruff designer. Graham Andrews was another customer, and an exacting one at that. Peter Cale, former Bruff engineer, remembers his demands for precision:

> When you did his machine, everything had to be spot on. He was meticulous. He wanted the blades to be razor sharp. He used to come around and say, "have you put that fag paper in there yet?" He knew that if you put a cigarette paper in and it sliced it through, it was sharp enough. Graham was happy then.

Fixing the Beast

The Hop Marketing Board's costing notebook for Messrs Gallimore and Parry of 1958 (see p. 44), illustrates the expensive demands of hop growing. The weekend ending 8 November, Mr M. Worgen spent 34 hours repairing the hop machine. Meanwhile, R. Allen, A. Hughes and J. Lilley spent a useful six hours 'straightening hop pegs'. Mr Worgen was back again for another eight hours of repairs to the hop machine. A week later a Mr T. Jones put in another 13 hours. And by the end of March a note was made, 'spares from Bruff for hop machine'. By July it was another four hours of Mr F. Mitchell's time and as the harvest beckoned, M. Worgen was back again for another nine hours 'overhauling the machine'. But a week later the ante was clearly upped with T. Jones spending 14 hours on it, W. Wactor 11 hours, J. Jones six hours, F. Mitchell 17 hours and back to M. Worgen, 21 hours.

Peter Cale was brought up in Suckley and still lives there today with his wife, Veronica, also an ex-Bruff worker. In 1959, aged 19, he started in the Bruff machine shop, joining another 100 fellow workers, travelling from Bromyard, Malvern, Cradley, on foot, bike or motorbike. He got to know the machine very well in all its forms, from the A-type (the first one), the B-Type, C-Type, E-Type or the F-Type, each one adopting improved levels of technology and engineering. The biggest was the Super E-Type:

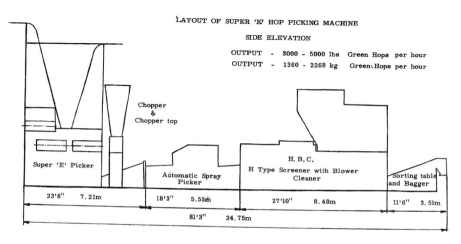

LAYOUT OF SUPER 'E' HOP PICKING MACHINE

SIDE ELEVATION

OUTPUT - 3000 - 5000 lbs Green Hops per hour
OUTPUT - 1360 - 2268 kg Green Hops per hour

Chopper & Chopper top

Super 'E' Picker

Automatic Spray Picker

H Type Screener with Blower Cleaner

H.B.C.

Sorting table and Bagger

23'8"   7.21m   18'3"   5.55m   27'10"   8.48m   11'6"   3.51m

81'3"   24.75m

Bruff picking machine being delivered by road, rail and ship (© John Griffiths)

Bruff was well-established when I joined in 1959. You could be doing 60/70 hours a week, at weekends, late at night. There was as much work as you wanted, especially towards the picking season because very often they were behind schedule. They were so busy. The machines had to be installed and I was one of the gangs that used to go out to get them finished, set up and ready to run before picking started. I was in the machine shop, but it got so busy that you were called on from any department.

We used to have to go down to Kent too. You'd have a fortnight there, stay until the job was done. The machine would go down in three sections, the picking unit, then the spray picker, then the screener or the cleaner at the end, as well as the auxiliary bits on the side, conveyers and all the tracking. We're talking about 30-odd ton of machinery to assemble and set up.

Peter went self-employed in 1981 (Bruff had been bought by CWF in the late 1970s), working alongside Fred Morris until he retired. Ninety per cent of their time was spent on Bruff machines. Meanwhile, growers coming out of hops left a trail of these mighty machines in their wake. Those not adopted, bought up and installed by other growers, were stripped for spare parts by Peter. He had a customer base of between 40 and 50, all hungry for recycled parts.

Left: a new hop-picking machine being installed at Brierley Court in 1980 by CWF, who bought out Bruff in the late 1970s. *Right*: Designer Robin Peers (*left*), and CWF Managing Director, R. Max Johnstone (*right*) (© Derek Evans/ HARC)

In 1980 I assembled three hop-picking machines that had come up from a Kent farmer who had packed up. They arrived in pieces, onto a slab of concrete at Eardiston. The worst thing was there were three different machines and they brought them up and threw them all in a pile in the yard and said, "we've got some film you can look at about the set-up in Kent". So I watched the film, got half-way through this video, and the chap said, "the bloody battery's packed up!" And that was it, went blank, and that's all I had. Basically, I was assembling three Bruff machines blindly. But I knew what models they were, E-Types, and that helped. The company were a bit late putting the concrete slabs down and when I got there to assemble the machines the farmers started pestering me because the picking season was just around the corner. I said, "just leave me alone and it will be finished, like I said, on the 29th of August". And that's exactly when I finished. It took several months, me and another fella, and when we pressed the button it came on!

Mobile communications in the 1980s were of course generally primitive, just first or second-class post or a lonely red telephone box dotted around the countryside. Peter's wife Veronica was at home fielding calls throughout the season, often from fraught farmers:

Peter would be at the farm working and I would be at home taking calls, "where is Peter? The machine has broken down, how long before he is here?" Peter would leave the farm where he was, find the nearest phone box, call me, and ask, "who's next on the list?" For the six weeks of picking it was a nightmare. The phone was constantly ringing with farmers wanting Peter. He'd leave early in the morning, be away all day, sometimes would be away all night, or the early hours of the morning, because machines had broken down and farmers wanted to get going again in the morning. Places like Paunton Court worked 24-hours a day. There was no rest.

FROM CRIBS TO FLYING BELTS — NO PLACE FOR CHILDREN ANY MORE
Despite mechanisation, some labour was still required, and some pickers still needed their fix. There is a poignancy to their determination to stick to old habits. Peter Walker:

We had some great old characters who just kept coming back to Ankerdine. They couldn't stop. This would have been the 1960s and they were the remnants of the old hand-pickers who came and sorted the leaves out on the machine. They came every year from Dudley until they died out basically. Black Country girls they were. There was one lady who did the rollers, she was the last of the South Wales' women. We still had

Left to right: Mrs Walker inspecting hops; women on the picking machine at Ankerdine (© Peter Walker); Black Country machine pickers in the 1960s (© George and Lil Hopkins)

the barracks and they stayed there, even sleeping on straw and cooking on an open devil. They kept coming back because they loved it, until they just fell off the perch one day and we never knew because they just stopped coming.

The labourers had to adapt to the new regime, as Neil Parker discovered:

In those days the machines were unguarded, with belts flying everywhere. We had a set of rollers that we had the women on, taking out the stalks and leaves all day. We had a ruction once when one of the girls got her hand stuck in the machine. We were pressing buttons all over the place and got her hand out. She nearly fainted, so Dad went and got her some brandy. Well of course they were all going down like flies then!

Where once children were easily accommodated around hop harvests, mechanisation brought new dangers. Early models in particular had their risks. Guards on picking-machines are integral today; however, they were not a legal requirement on early versions, leading to some gruesome deaths and accidents. Tragedy struck in September 1958 when 16-year-old Gwen Reynolds died after becoming stuck in a picking machine at Pigeon House Farm, Weston Beggard. She was working with a team of 12, including her mother, when the accident happened.

In 1956 Kidderminster MP Gerald Nabarro spoke out in the House of Commons during the Agriculture Safety, Health and Welfare Provisions Bill following the fatal accident at a hop farm in his constituency. During the harvest a Ludlow woman had been fatally injured working on a picking machine. She had ignored a warning to wear a cap and had been scalped when her hair was caught in a roller.

The picking machine marked a sea-change for everyone, especially mothers. They had been used to bringing their children to work, the little ones placed in cribs; the older ones watched over by their siblings. Mechanisation and increasing health and safety regulation, saw a decline in the presence of women in the hop harvest. Children and machines just did not mix.

Yet Monica Symonds wasn't fazed. She adapted to mechanisation with gusto. For her there was little change and she would bring her six-month-old daughter still, tucked away in her pram: 'Someone used to shout, "Monica!

This page: The hop picking machine at Instone Court (© Laura Haworth). *Opposite page, clockwise from top right*: Machine pickers at Coopers Farm, Knighton on Teme (© Jessie Dallow); Hop bines being fed into the hop machine at Instone Court (© Laura Haworth); Hops arriving at the machine shed at Ankerdine (© Peter Walker); Polish workers inside and outside the machine shed at Yarkhill Court, and planning their route home (© Michael Leigh)

She's awake!" She was always fine. We used to have to hang the bines on, sweeping the mess up and throwing it in the back of the machine. It was a lot harder work than hand-picking, and you missed all the excitement too.'

The arrival of the first picking machine alarmed Lil Hopkins. Gone were the days of scratting, chatter and singing in the hopyards, children playing, and babies nestled in hops. Lil:

> It was a bit frightening because it was so big. I remember when the first one came, my daughter was only a baby and it changed everything, but it was much easier too. You had to be careful because it was dangerous. You couldn't have children running around, so she was in a pram. They were so big these machines, people used to get their fingers caught up. But she was very good in the pram. She would stop right at the bottom of the row while I was at the top. It was lovely bringing children to work, you had to, but it changed when the machines came.

Changes affected by mechanisation were felt in other areas too. *The Tewkesbury Register & Agriculture Gazette* featured a story from a local printing firm in 1954 about their state of affairs:

> Many of my customers of former years no longer need books and tallies that were so essential a part of the picking season, and over the last five years the sales of these items have slowly decreased until this year, when I have sold practically none at all. How true the old saying "one man's gain is another man's loss." Year after year we live to see changes, but may we never live to see the day when someone introduces us to mechanical drinking!

6

Drying the Hop:
'where the magic happens'

The kiln was where it was all at. I'm telling you, those buildings came alive during hop-picking, the sheer character of them. They're ordinary buildings most of the year, but for two weeks hop picking, those kilns come alive. It's where the magic happens.

Ray Morris, Burton Mill Farm, Shropshire

THE drying of hops is arguably the most important and prized job on a hop farm. What happens within a kiln is hidden from sight and the process is imbued with an air of mystery – and indeed the drying of hops was always an uncertain science, reliant on touch, smell, experience and an uncanny sense of when the time was right. In the wrong hands, drying could go awry with costly consequences. The head kiln dryer was often a hereditary position, sons learning from fathers. While the drying period was an intense six-weeks, a marathon run, all eyes on the finishing line, little rest or sleep, remaining alert and vigilant at all times.

THE WORKINGS OF THE KILN

The architecture of the kiln defines our hop-growing area, its vernacular a part of our local identity and regional difference. These singular structures have seen countless tons of hops pass through, the hops' essential oils impregnating the woodwork and brickwork. Often red-bricked, some round, more often square, sometimes half-timbered, their tall cone-shaped roofs stand out, like windmills on the horizon. These buildings are reminders of a farming heritage, yet they were once at the cutting-edge of agricultural developments. They were a very practical solution for the grower, providing specialised drying facilities for hops. Most old-style kilns continued in use

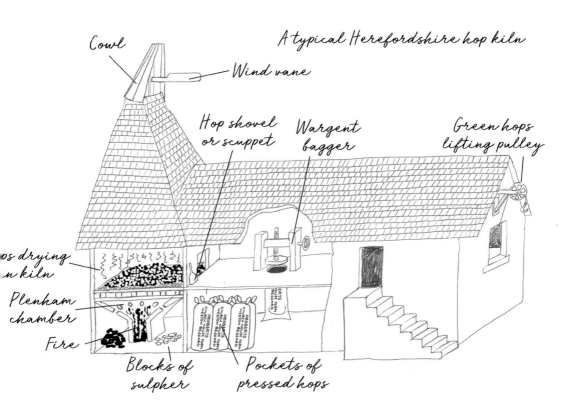

Labels on drawing:
Cowl

A typical Herefordshire hop kiln

Wind vane

Hop shovel or scuppet

Wargent bagger

Green hops lifting pulley

os drying n kiln

Plenham chamber

Fire

Blocks of sulpher

Pockets of pressed hops

Drawing of a typical Herefordshire hop kiln (© John Symonds)

until they became either not large enough or unsuitable for adaptation, and were eventually replaced by entirely new state-of-the-art structures equipped with the latest technology.

The kiln was a warm and muggy place, often sweaty and filled with the pungent aroma ever-present. Some loved it, others hated it. Inside the kiln, sounds were muffled, any noise absorbed by the hops, the brickwork, wooden beams and the sacking. Meanwhile, the walls and the skin, hair, clothes and boots of the dryer absorbed the resin of the hop. There was an exclusivity to the kiln too. It was a members-only club. You had to know the business of a kiln to warrant entry here, understand the code: watchful, alert, attentive, one load in, the other out, another cooling, all at just the right moment. Too dry, and the hops could self-combust; too damp and they could go mouldy. Drying hops was a tactile business. The dryer would bury his hands into the drying hops, bringing them to his nose, sniffing, then rubbing them between his hands, more rubbing: were they dry enough? A bit longer?

Opposite: A pair of round hop kilns near Mathon (© Philip Halling, Geograph)

Top: The Haven, near Dilwyn, originally had a pair of round hop kilns, seen here in the first half of the twentieth century (© Carol and Edward Lewis). *Above*: These were replaced *c.*1950 with a single, larger rectangular kiln (© R. Wheeler)

Above: Larport Farm, near Mordiford (© R. Wheeler). *Below, clockwise from top left*: Avenbury Court (© Andy Johnson); Ankerdine (© Laura Haworth); hop kiln near Shucknall (© R. Wheeler); Walsopthorne Farm has two capped kilns, one round and one square (© Duncan James); The Sponend, Fromes Hill, in 1949 (© Janet Parker)

Dick Helme worked the kilns at Southfield Farm, Canon Frome for the Payne family in the 1940s. He could do the job blindfolded:

The tractors hauled the hops in the trailers to the farmyard to the green stage, then the sacks were put on a conveyor belt ready to load into the kiln for drying. In the kiln, six hessian nets, or we called them the hairs, were attached around the walls of the kiln above the slatted floor. The hops were loaded onto the hessian nets to about two-foot-six inches deep and they were levelled out so that they would dry evenly. The kiln doors were then shut, and sulphur was put in a tray in the basement below, where the burners were. We would set fire to the sulphur and once well and truly alight, we'd get out, shut the door and start the fans up, which blew the sulphur up through the slatted floors into the hops. When it had burnt out the drying process would begin, which took about eight hours.

Judy Helme,
Hops'n'Hoptons, 2001

Top: Loading green sacks onto a dray in a hopyard (© Miss White). *Above*: The green stage at Ankerdine with kiln men with scuppets and bushel baskets (© Peter Walker)

Kiln man forking hops in the kiln at Ankerdine (© Peter Walker)

Kiln man pausing for a photograph while spreading hops ready for drying in a Worcestershire hop kiln in 1934 (© Georgina Wheeler)

Stanford Court kiln man, Bill Lewis (aka 'the Colonel') readying hops for drying in a round kiln (© Robert Jones)

The irony when you are drying hops is that, while you are working very long days, you are also dealing with a plant that makes you want to go to sleep! There is something we call hop farmer's syndrome: the first week you are keen, the second week you are tired, and the third week you really don't care, and after that the body just adjusts and you just carry on. Simon Parker, Instone Court

Hop drying, despite the debilitating tiredness, was also a social time, with family, friends and sometimes strangers dropping in at all hours of the night — not that they were always welcome. There was always someone around. Geoff Thompson's last harvest at Little Lambswick Farm, Lindridge, was in 2018:

> I have always enjoyed the fact that hops involve lots of people and you can build a great team. So harvesting, although extremely hard work, there was also a great camaraderie in the team, and that became even more rewarding when the crop was finally in. We always had a bit of a party when we finished. Usually we needed approximately 20 people at picking time, most of these were locals with whom we built up a close friendship and a hardcore of that team stayed with us for many years. We have always had so many good evenings in the kilns. We usually had no trouble getting extra help for evening kiln-loading as there was always good fun, banter aided by ample home-made Oldfields Cider.
>
> There is nothing quite like the amazing smell of hops when they are drying or dried on the kiln floor. To go up into the kilns early in the morning and take in that wonderful aroma, was quite special. It's been a pleasure to have an excellent team to help me harvest my 40 hop crops. Roger Bray has been exceptional in his skill at drying the hops for me.

Roger Bray is a kiln master. His experience and skill in the kiln at Lambswick Farm have won him numerous trophies and titles, both at local and national levels. He has been part of the fabric there for 68 years, following his teacher and mentor, his father Reg into the drying rooms. He knows instinctively when hops are properly dried:

> When I was eight I'd be home from Lindridge school, change my clothes, and run to the kiln straight away – that's where all my learning was. Many a time I'd be there at night helping him load the kilns and Mum used to

come shouting, "Roger! School in the morning!" I loved it. I learned a lot from Dad. He would say, "go and have a look at that kiln, they shouldn't be too far off now", that sort of thing. You can tell by the feel, rubbing them for the moisture content. We don't have any instruments. It's in your blood and hop picking is a way of life.

When drying you have to consider the variety. I used to dread doing the new varieties and was wary of them. I'd been used to the old Goldings and Fuggles. Fuggles are my favourite. You knew when to go and start looking at them, seven hours. But Northdown, Northern Brewer, they were ten hours. You wanted anything between ten and eleven per cent moisture content; twelve you could get away with. It's a fine balance. It's all done by touch.

Hops drying with kiln door closed
(© Miss White)

Roger was so dedicated to the cause of hop-drying that he even risked the ire of one of his old employers:

When I left school I worked for an engineering firm on a universal milling machine, but I would still take time off for the harvest. But one year they wouldn't let me take leave so I got Mum to ring one Monday morning to say I had a bad back. So then I was in the kilns with Dad all week. When I went back to work the Monday morning the lads knew where I'd been and they had decorated my machine, covering it in hops! My foreman said we knew where you were!

Dried hops being shovelled out of the kiln, now ready for pocketing
(© Miss White)

Top: Ernie Johnstone, Bill Lewis and Richard Potter in Stanford Court kiln (© Robert Jones). *Middle*: in the kiln at the Grange (© Andrews family). *Below*: A full kiln at Instone Court (© Laura Haworth)

The art of drying was almost reverential at times. To those never allowed over the threshold, the culture of the kiln was something of a mystery. Often, the skill of a hop dryer was passed down the family line, lessons beginning early on, spending time with older, experienced men, watching, listening, observing, learning. Mervyn Carless acquired his skills in a similar way, from Trevor Woonton at Woodmanton:

> The hop dryer was quite a revered person. There was a sort of myth around people who dried hops because what they did was quite an art. The growers were not allowed upstairs at all. Trevor taught me the skill of hop drying; you learn by experience. And, of course, every hop grower has got a different system. He showed me the basics, putting your hand in just below the surface and, as we called it, rubbing the hops out. He was a good teacher.
>
> He never drank alcohol so there was no drink in the kiln. The older generation would have cider or beer. You were hot all the time and it would take about three weeks to recover from 24-hour hop drying. We had a bed in what was like an old cow shed and played cards half-way through the night. We used to do two hours on, two hours off.

For some dryers, cider was readily available: 'You usually had to break your sleep in the middle of the night to unload the kiln. A big barrel of cider was always ordered from Westons' Cider for the kiln workers and it didn't take long to empty it!'

Growers often find it difficult to explain the skills of the hop dryer. Maybe they do not want to share their secrets. 'You could write a book on the secrecy of growers,' said Tom Probert. Tom grows hops at Church House Farm and talks of the:

> dark magic in the kiln! We're all after the same end-product and we've all got very different ways of getting there. It's peculiar. We've had some Spanish growers here who want some absolute measurable way of getting hops off the kiln. "Well, you just grab a handful and rub them and ..." But, then they say, "what do you mean?" "Well you just feel them!" We are very sophisticated bits of kit. The kiln is really where it's all make or break.

Second World War veteran Ernest Breakwell (*right*) drying hops at Tenbury (© Brian Breakwell)

The grower chooses his dryer carefully, returning again and again to an old and trusted worker. It is a wise grower who accepts that, in the kiln, it is the dryer who is king and not the grower. Bill Morris dried hops at Newhouse Farm as a young man and claims most farm workers in his day were 'employed by sight and not by sound!' Ray Morris:

> A hop dryer is a very specialised job and a very skilful one too. My son can do it now, but most dryers don't reach their peak until they're in their fifties. Not just anyone can come in. He's the most important man in the kiln – he's in charge, not me. He knows how many sacks he wants that night, and he's the one who tells you when the hops are dry. So he's in charge. No doubt about it. The dryer could put his hand in, rub the hops, and tell you when they were ready.
>
> I used to go and help at night and we would change the one kiln at about 11 or 12 o'clock at night, pull the hops off, turn the burner off and blow cool air through to get them down to about 100 degrees. Then they were pulled off in hairs and tipped in the cooling room, then the hairs put back on in the kiln again and then we carried the sacks of green hops and tipped them in and the dryer usually had a long-handled fork which he'd lighten them up with. Had to be really forked up to get the air around it. Oh yes, there's an art to it alright.

Before the arrival of oil- and gas-fired burners, hop growers were dependent on coal for drying hops. Haulage of this heavy load was by teams of horses and wagons, and even barges on the Rivers Severn and Wye at one time. Some growers in Herefordshire collected theirs from the Forest of Dean. If conditions were right, barges deposited this black gold at quays along the River Wye. South Wales' coal was also used. Pensax Pits in Worcestershire supplied fuel for many farms in the eastern part of the region. The Baiting House Inn at Sapey is said to have earned its name from being the popular stopping-off point for wagoners and their team of horses, who called in for food on their way to and from the pits. The opening of the railways in the 1850s ushered in dramatic changes, and hauling fuel by horse and barge rapidly declined. John Thacker of Upper Sapey well remembers the ordeal of coal haulage:

A lot of people think the Baiting Inn, our local pub in Upper Sapey, has to do with baiting animals. It is not. In Herefordshire 'bait' means food and when the local hop farmers used to fetch their open-cast coal from Menith Wood, the Inn was where they used to stop for bait for their horses and themselves. Unlike the Welsh coal, Menith was a second-quality coal which burned slower and seemed to suit the hop drying. The coal used to be loaded, by hand of course, and it seemed to get loaded quicker if they took along a barrel of cider.

One day when Dick Benbow's father, Walter, was a lad, around 1911, he was told he'd got to go with the coal carters on a job. Although he didn't want to go, he had to, rolling around in the empty cart from Burley Gate to Menith Wood, which is a long way. He still didn't know what he was supposed to do when they had loaded the coal. But when they reached Stanford Bank the wagoner got in the hedge and cut the long, swishy nut stick and put young Walter on top of the coal with the swishy stick. The reason was the horses had to have a quarter of an hour rest at two places on the Bank because it was such a long, steep, heavy haul. And while the horses were rested the women from Sapey Common used to come out to pinch the coal. Walter's job was to beat them back! If you got up the Stanford Bank now you can still see the level places on the road where they used to stop.

John Griffiths is a retired haulier from Suckley. Today he lives a few hundred metres from the family's old redbrick coke-fired kiln. It was last used in the 1940s and remains today as it was the last time hops went in. The cowl is still in place, the cast iron coke door too. At the entrance, several scythes hang from the wall. The wooden steps are falling away, but upstairs in the drying room the slats are still visible and the remains of the hairs are still hooked onto the wall. John isn't sentimental, however; it's just another building as far as he is concerned. But for the working dryer, the kiln was their dominion. John:

> Hop dryers wouldn't let anyone in because it was their territory and they were doing an important job. Whoever was the dryer, their fathers had probably been one too; it was an inheritance job. They literally didn't go home for six weeks. It's all done by computer now, but then it was all done by touch; not too dry and not too wet. The old ones used to have a pen-knife, so they could press it into the pocket and they could tell by the feel of the hops if they were too wet or too dry; it's like a woman doing a cake, you put a skewer into it to see if it's cooked or not. If not quite ready, they would put them back in the kiln. Some farmers were always having to re-dry their hops because the dryers were not reliable. You had to choose your dryer carefully.

One of the oldest hop kilns in the region, a seventeenth-century stone and timber-framed kiln at Church House Farm, Weston Beggard, burned to the ground in 2015. Tom Probert checked the kiln at 1am:

> I went back again at 3am and it was already burnt to the floor, by 6am it was just cinder, nothing left. But we still had hops to pick and dry so we were on the phone and by 10am that morning we were picking hops again and taking them down the road to Charles Pudge in Bishops Frome, who very kindly offered his kilns to us. Couldn't thank him enough. It was devastating, but at the time we had a valuable crop and we had to get on and do something.

The hop community responded generously to the plight at Little Lambswick Farm, Lindridge, in 1982 when Geoff Thompson had a kiln fire:

We were only part way through our picking. But the wonderful thing with such a small band of farmers growing the same crop and being aware of the consequences of such a disaster, is that they tended to all help each other out when a problem occurred. In our case, the Spilsbury family from Orleton came to our rescue when they had finished picking, and the Godsell family from Stretton Grandison lent us their kilns. We also hired kilns from the Powell-Tuck family at Ashperton. It was a lot of work to haul the hops in green sacks to Hereford, but all the hops were safely gathered in the end.

Hop Fire!

Kiln fires were dreaded but were not unusual. When they did occur, the hop community responded and didn't waste time in finding a solution for their fellow affected grower. Philip Price:

I was in the hopyard and I could hear all this banging going on and I thought they were clay pigeon shooting and thought, "I'm working my socks off and they're clay pigeon shooting!" So I rushed up to have a look and saw the asbestos exploding off the roof of the kilns. It was a mess. We were hauling the hops over to Cowarne Court for the drying after that. The kiln was completely destroyed.

(© Derek Evans/ HARC)

Georgina Wheeler was named after her father, George Seaborn. He was head dryer at Ivington Bury Farm, Leominster. The kilns are still there, although hops are no longer grown. She remembers how during the drying season there was no time for family time. On Sundays during the drying marathon, she was under strict instructions to be as quiet as a mouse since it was the only day of the week her father slept in his own bed away from the kiln. Sometimes during the week, however, she was allowed to see him:

A scuppet and heaped hops at Instone Court (© Laura Haworth)

There were another five men in the kiln with him. He was the top man. He had to make sure all the fires and the temperature was right in all three kilns. They didn't get much sleep and were always on call. Three would be awake and three would sleep. At nine in the evening I was allowed to go and see him for five minutes before bedtime because I wanted to see him and also to watch the hops go down the chute into the hop pocket. On Sundays he spent all day in bed. I was told to be quiet because he needed his sleep. When us kids went to the kiln to see our dads we used to lie on their beds. They were big straw beds with sacking over the top and around the sides and you'd get these rats around. He had to tie his trousers around the bottom otherwise he'd have them running up his legs! We loved it. Mr Ernest Speakman, the owner, was very good. He used to say, "if the children want to see their dads, I'm not stopping them".

They weren't given alcohol in the kiln because they could get drunk and they had a big responsibility, but they did have flasks of tea to keep them awake. The heat in there was so intense they got really tired and just wanted to sleep. In the middle of the night, once he'd checked the kilns, he would go walking around the fields just to get some fresh air, then come back in an hour and check it again and then go out for another walk. If he fell asleep and something went wrong that was his responsibility. At the end of the drying season, Mother used to put his clothes in the boiler in the washhouse outside and boil them up. We had no money for new clothes, so they had to be used again.

THE PRIMROSE EFFECT: BURNING SULPHUR

When hops are being dried in kilns, a quantity of sulphur (in the form of a roll of Brimstone) is invariably burnt beneath them during the first two or three hours of the drying. The fumes of burnt sulphur (sulphur dioxide) pass through the hops and by their passage bleach the hops. The amount of sulphur used is usually about ½ lb to 10 bushels of green hops, or approximately, 5lb of sulphur to 1 pocket of hops. If the hops are very green when picked, as much as double this quantity is used. 'The Uses of Sulphur in the Cultivation and Curing of Hops', Arthur Amos BA, 1909

The practise of treating hops with sulphur at the start of the drying process was introduced in the 1790s, primarily to give freshly-picked hop cones the 'primrose' effect, a brighter, fresher look, reducing decolourisation during the drying period. It was still being used up until 1980, when, under instructions from the Hop Marketing Board, and at the request of the Brewer's Society, growers stopped using it. This was a relief to hop dryers, who uniformly cursed the 'yellow mist'. Edward Lewis' family at Eggleton Court 'used to use tons of it. The air was blue most of the time. It would tighten your chest up and get rid of your zits!'

Sulphur was smelly, noxious and treacherous too. Janet Parker of Stoke Lacy remembers its perils on her parents' farm:

> Lighting the sulphur was a dangerous job because methylated spirits were tipped into a special iron pan that contained the sulphur and then it was lit with a match. But you couldn't see it was lit. I had a friend who was killed as he thought the sulphur hadn't been lit so he tipped some more meths on and it blew back up the bottle and he was very badly burned and died three weeks later. It was a sad lesson for all hop dryers.

Growers had different routines to avoid such accidents. Peter Walker has been caught out and quickly learned by it: 'You can't see meths burning until you realise your sleeve is alight. Once that's happened once or twice, you learn to wet your sleeves before you go in.'

Another primitive health and safety practise was the so-called 'horse-shoe effect'. The kiln stoker at Millend, for example, kept horse shoes in the kiln brazier and when they were red hot, removed them and threw them into the tray of sulphur. It was a safe way to ignite the sulphur. The dryers broadly welcomed the eventual sulphur ban, although some old-timers took a while to acclimatise to the change, as Clive Wheatstone learned at Dormington in the 1980s:

> If the hops took a long time to cook then you had the chance to go down the pub. The thing used to be that when you came out of the kiln you had a pint of cider because it was supposed to kill off the effects of the sulphur. Even though it was the first year without sulphur, there was still a barrel of cider next to the kiln.

Bill Morris has been up to his knees in hops since the 1950s, at Newhouse Farm. It was a coke-fired kiln in the early days, excellent for baking potatoes in the hot ashes, extracting when softened and slathered in farmhouse butter. Sulphur, though, presented other problems that could only be resolved by someone with a head for heights – in this case, a fearless Bill Morris:

> Some farmers used to light the sulphur and go to the next farm and wait for the smell to go over. At Newhouse, when we got electric in the fifties, the sulphur used to go out through the fans and then get on the motor and that would make you cough and spit. So you would have to sandpaper it off, otherwise it would make the fan stop, and you needed the fan to keep the air circulating. So I had to get up a 40-foot ladder to the top of the kiln to scrape the sulphur off. Can you imagine? I had no choice. It had to be done.

Georgina Wheeler's father, George, suffered more than most from the effects of sulphur:

> He was washing his feet in Epsom salts because the sulphur was burning through his boots and he had big holes in his feet. After six weeks of drying he could hardly walk. There was no health and safety, just strong boots, no masks or goggles. You could hardly get your breath in there. During the drying he smelt to the high heavens. All he had time for was to swill his face in a bowl of Epsom salts. Mum would give him a hot drink and a cheese sandwich to see him through the night.

FOUR SQUARE MEALS A DAY

Farmers' wives launched a culinary campaign from their kitchens during drying time. The men in the kiln were well-fed and never allowed to go hungry or thirsty, receiving a good, hearty four meals a day. Kilns of old were once attached to farmhouses with easy access to the kitchens and food. From first light, it was a solid fry-up, cups of sweet tea; a few hours later and lunchtime, steak and kidney pie, potatoes and carrots, more sweet tea and maybe the added pleasure of a glass of sweet, cold farmhouse cider; teatime cottage pie with a hunk of bread followed by a slice of apple

Bait time at Yarkhill Court (© Michael Leigh)

pie covered in generous lashings of farmhouse cream; sweet tea again. Then, as darkness descended, and stomachs rumbled, the last meal of the day, more bread, cheese, pickle, salad onions, pork pie, a piece of freshly-baked Victoria sponge, washed down with a blessed glass of cider.

Their catering was both heroic in scale and demand, and a welcome sight to these tired men working 24-hours a day in the kiln. Although it varied from farm to farm, they might also have to look after their pickers, providing tea from the back of a wagon, fuel for the hop devils, faggots of wood, oil for lamps, or manage the farmhouse shop, selling eggs, flour, bread and potatoes.

Lambswick master dryer Roger Bray lived at Mayfields Farm, Hammonds Frome, until the age of ten, where his father worked the hops. The owner, Miss Matthews lived closer than most to the hops during harvest time:

> She lived in the big house. The hop room was above the kitchen and the pocket hole went down into the kitchen, where they used to do the bagging. She used to have to move out of the kitchen because they used to do the pocketing there and the pockets were kept in there too because they didn't grow much acreage. I remember that.

DEVOTION TO DUTY

Edward Smith was the ill-fated Captain of the Titanic. After striking an iceberg in 1912, the liner sank, taking Smith with it. For his stoicism and fortitude in the face of adversity, Smith has become an icon of British spirit and discipline. As far from the sea and the Titanic as he could possibly be, was George Green of Ankerdine. Hop dryers are noted for their devotion to duty, but George took his responsibilities to extremes. In 1946 the River Teme flooded, engulfing Ankerdine's hopyards. It was harvest time and George was doing what he did best, drying the hops and ignoring the inclement conditions. Even as the flood waters washed through the kilns, George refused to abandon 'his ship' and remained glued to his chair. Eventually, after frantic appeals from fellow workers, he was forcibly carried in his chair to safety. He would have been relieved to learn that some hops survived, and the harvesting and drying soon snapped back into action.

BAGGING HOPS

The kiln was, for the most part, a male domain. Yet, some women slipped through the net. Terry Chandler worked on an Ivington hop farm in the 1960s, bagging hops with a mechanical press that demanded brute strength to operate. Terry took on a young Gypsy man to help, but in the busy atmosphere at hop-time, he was not helpful:

> I was pulling 300-weight on the bagger. It needed a lot of strength, but he couldn't pull as much. This went on for a couple of weeks and I couldn't work out why. And then one day I was walking through the hopyard and I caught 'him' going to the toilet in the hop rows: he was a she! Teresa was her name and she had dressed up as a man to get more money. I just never cottoned on. After that she went back to picking hops as normal.

Dried hops, once cooled to the right temperature, were spread out on the bagging room floor, and, using a wooden shovel called a 'scuppet', were pushed through a hole into the pocket suspended below. Before the invention of the mechanical press, some unfortunate man had the job of standing in the pocket for hours on end, pressing the hops down with his feet. Although he was kept supplied with cider to keep his throat clear, it was hot, dusty work. A hand-operated plunger that pressed down on the hops until the pocket was full and tightly compacted, eventually took his place. Further advancements were made by Harold Edwards of Collington with his design for the electrically-powered plunger in the 1950s.

Hop growing at The Grange, Bosbury, took place under the watchful eye of Graham Andrews. He mentored several younger growers, who all learnt a valuable lesson from him: attention to detail at all times. By Graham's side was his wife Barbara, 83, a woman never afraid to get her hands dirty. She was driving a tractor long before it was usual for a woman to do so, drawing curious glances from workers on other farms. She was there at drying time too, hauling hops into the kiln, and out again:

> I was knackered at the end of the season, but we thought nothing of it. My favourite part was the end! I liked getting down to the hopyard and seeing how much left there was to do and how much longer it was going to be. You only did eight or ten rows a day. If the hops came off the kiln at 12, we would be bagging by six. I used to do the bagging with Carol, our daughter, pushing the hops in. Carol could operate the press. Even when we were bagging we would still be checking the hops to see if they were dried enough, put your hand in, have a rub. Graham would always say, "have you checked them?" Oh, I loved it.

Barbara Andrews and husband Graham (on the press) at The Grange (© Andrews family)

Pressing hops into pockets (© Brian Willder)

Clockwise from above: Graham Andrews at The Grange (© Andrews family); Pocketing hops in Herefordshire kiln c.1940s (© Miss White); Ernie Hall toggling pockets at The Grange (© Andrews family); Rob Hancock and his sister Susan Vaughan at Wyercroft, Bishops Frome (© M. O'Mahony); Richard Potter at Stanford Court (© Robert Jones); the press at Instone Court, being operated by Adrian Toma (© Laura Haworth)

Tom Nellist's father was manager at Leighton Court, where the bagging was left in the capable hands of a Welshman:

> The dryer wouldn't bag the dried hops. That was done by a Welsh miner called Billy Newton. He came up from Tredegar every year just to do the bagging. It was his annual holiday. We used a mechanised hand-press, pressing the hops into the old pockets. A big plunger went down on a ratchet, but if you put too much pressure on the pocket it would rip. You had to judge it just right and it took a lot of skill to get it spot on. It was an experienced role for an experienced man, like Billy Newton.

A pressed pocket of hops is an unwieldy and unyielding object. It is heavy, giving very little room for leverage and packed hard like concrete. Some of the simplest and most useful tools in the bagging room are the bagging hooks, used to lift and move the pockets. Woe betide anyone who mislays them. With no artifice, they are knocked into shape by the local blacksmith, and often passed down the generations, but they can easily get lost. Simon Parker of Instone Court, lost his once, leading to great panic. After a search, they were found, sewn up in a pocket!

Loading pockets into a lorry at Yarkhill Court (© Michael Leigh)

A new hop bale press, the Trumpet Bale Press, has been launched by C.W.F. Engineering of Ledbury. Traditionally, hops are packed in pockets but more growers are moving to the use of the bale press because of substantial savings in raw material packaging costs and the shape, which is more suitable for storage and mechanical handling. It can produce up to ten bales per hour. Journal of the Hop Marketing Board, Spring 1982

Ernie Hall sewing hop pockets at The Grange (© Andrews family)

Hop pockets were emblematic of the industry, but they are gradually being phased out in favour of hop bales. There are a few who continue to use pockets, but the move to bales is driven by economics and logistics. Richard Phillips at Eggleton Court changed over to bales in the 2010s:

> Pockets were a lot harder work and very difficult to manoeuvre. I have
> fond memories of them, but I don't miss moving them around. It's all
> computerised now and we use a RB60 baler. The bale comes out like
> a pea-in-a-pod, each weighing 60 kilos, and easy to put onto a pallet.
> Simple. A lot of the manual handling has gone out of the business of hops
> and that's a good thing.

John Walker's farm at Tedney straddles the Herefordshire–Worcestershire border. He grows dwarf hops on one side of the border and organic varieties on the other, and he also uses 60-kilo bales, although he started off with something much heavier:

> We used to make 80-kilo bales. They are a fair old lump to lift on your shoulders, but much better than our old pockets. We had to stitch these bales down the sides and if the stitcher broke and we were running fairly close to capacity, the system stopped all for want of a stitcher! And there isn't room to store the hops until they are baled. The stitcher is just like a sewing machine; you put a sheet above and a sheet below the hops and stitch the sides and that creates the bale. They come as socks now, but you used to get bolts of cloth and have to cut them to length and stencil them and then sew them in the shed. Socks are much easier.

Left: Mervyn Carless taking hop samples from baled hops (© Mervyn Carless).
Right: Baling hops at Tedney (© Peter Walker)

Ingenious or unorthodox methods were sometimes required to start the engines that drove the kiln's heaters. One Worcestershire grower used a gun cartridge, without the lead shot, to start a Blackstone engine:

> We found that it would fire that way and hopefully start the engine over. But they had run out of cartridges this one time, so someone had the bright idea of using a 12-bore cartridge. They were supposed to have taken the shot out but hadn't. It just blasted out. No one was injured, but it did start the engine!

Such methods would never be used in state-of-the-art modern hop kilns. Far removed from the vernacular red-brick or timber-framed buildings of old, these custom-built, cavernous, fabricated, steel-beamed agricultural buildings nevertheless house the kilns of the twenty-first century.

The first grower in the country to have a three-tier drying system with completely automatic loading was R. Capper Senior of Stocks Farm, Suckley. Others have followed and three or four-tier drying systems are increasingly common. Controlled by mobile phone app technology, they produce a constant stream of data for the grower: airflow, pressure differential, temperature controls, moisture content probes. Drying hops has reached the modern age. Old habits die hard, however, when it comes to competition time.

The kiln at Wyercroft Farm, Bishops Frome (© M. O'Mahony)

7

Hop Competitions: societies & sampling

As was anticipated, the hops were a fine sample. Seventeen lots were sent, and were fairly well dried, doing credit to the various men employed.

Tenbury Agriculture Show Hop Competition, October 1911

I N the weeks following the hop harvest, competition is gearing up. The pressure is off and there is time for some rest and relaxation. At the gate, money is collected, programmes handed over and you are directed to a parking space over bumpy ground to a field beyond. The days are getting shorter and there is a crispness in the air. In the fields the ploughmen and ploughwomen, seated in tractors or with teams of horses, have arrived early and the competition has started. Regulation tweed and flat caps in place, the ridge and furrows are observed with all the attention of an Olympic final.

Close by, another friendly battle is being fought in the marquees or barns that have been commandeered for the produce show. The fruits of the country-side – apples, pears, cabbages, red onions, carrots, parsnips, 21 categories in all – are arranged neatly on white paper plates. Women committee members in starched white coats, oversee the operation. In the corner, home-cooked food is prepared, with plenty of beer and cider. But to the far side, tucked away in a corner, is another category. There are a number of small, square-shaped packages, wrapped in a blue blotting-like paper. This paper is very important and expensive – it shields the hops from any daylight getting into the sample, that could change the colour of the hops. It is secured with a single brass upholstery pin. These are the hop samples. It is competition time.

The West Midlands holds three hop competitions. The match hosts are, in order of age: the Tenbury Agricultural Society (est. 1858), the Ledbury Ploughing Society (est. 1898) and the youngest, the Trumpet & District

Hop judging time at the 2019 Trumpet & District Agricultural Society's annual Ploughing Match, Coddington. L to R: Henry Rogers, Richard Bradstock, Edward Lewis, Steve Wright (the last certified hop propagator in the UK) and John Pudge of the Hop Pocket (© M. O'Mahony)

Agricultural Society (est. 1944). Their matches are a glorious evocation of another England, a paean to the countryside, rural life and farming. On display is the skill and dedication that brings food to our plates and beer to our tankards. Competition simmers politely under the surface. Representations from the brewing industry may be fewer these days, but it does no harm at all getting one's hops noticed here. The golden days of these hop contests may be behind us, but it's important to make an impression as the judges prowl.

THE SOCIETIES

The running order of the matches remains unaltered from year to year. Whether by design or not, Ledbury always takes place first, followed by Trumpet, and bringing up the rear, Tenbury, where the overall champion from the previous two hop sampling competitions is awarded a silver salver courtesy of E.L. Lewis & Son. It is an impressive award that would make a statement on anyone's sideboard. It joins other weighty and costly displays of silverware (certainly not silver plate) the three societies have accumulated over the centuries. The historic and lucrative nature of hop growing is manifested in these glinting displays, the most valuable cups are still awarded

Hop judging at the 2017 Trumpet & District Agriculture Society's annual Ploughing Match, Church House Farm, Weston Beggard. Hop growers, John Probert and son Tom, are second and third from right respectively. (© Clova Perez-Corral/ Herefordshire Life Through a Lens)

for hops. Some are trophies in memory of a son or father from hop-growing families lost in the wars. The Rimmell Memorial Cup, from the Ledbury Society, is a lasting example, dedicated to a family member at Pridewood, Ashperton, early last century, and is still awarded today.

Alistair Young is a former hop grower from Ledbury and the secretary of the Ledbury Ploughing Society. In the Society's early days, show categories included sheep management, wagoner skills and the art of pole pitching, 'who shall pitch no less than 2,000 stocks of hops'. Today, the number of entrants to the hop competitions has declined (as they have with the other societies, a sign of the dwindling number of growers), but competition is healthily strong, a hangover from the days when sales or contracts could be secured at these events. In those days, guests and judges included merchants and brewers. Alistair:

> People really wanted to win the classes they were eligible in. They still do, because they are mainly judged by people involved with the brewing industry, brewers or hop merchants. If you get mentioned in dispatches, if you like, it is good for your future sales; people in the trade look at the results and write them down, and people looking for quality hops take notice.

The 1955 Ledbury Match and Show was held 'by kind permission of Messrs H. Weston & Sons' at The Bounds and Nuttall, Much Marcle. The day's events were followed by dinner at the Feathers Hotel in Ledbury. Companies donating prizes came from across the hop industry, including: Messrs Brandram Bros & Co., merchants of Rotherhithe; supplier of hop requisites John Hill, Ledbury; Messrs Pan Brittanica Industries Ltd, an agrochemical company; hop-picking machine manufacturers George Hinds Ltd, Malvern; and Messrs Charles H. Bevan & Son, Borough High Street, hop factor.

At the inaugural Trumpet match in 1944, Mr W.J. Rimmell of Pridewood swept the board, winning eight first prizes including prize for best sample in the show. He was a stalwart of the society and later went on to judge the hop competition for many years. Over the years the changing programme categories offer a snapshot of an industry developing and adapting. In 1944 there were classes for hand-picked and machine-picked hops. By 1969, classes for new varieties including Northern Brewer and Bullion, and in 1996, the

HOPS

Chief Steward : Mr. N. A. J. Williams.

The W. J. Rimell Hop Cup and Classes 36, 37, 38 and 39 are open to growers throughout the United Kingdom.

No Sample is eligible for more than one Class.

Any Sample which in the opinion of the Judges has not been drawn from a genuinely bagged pocket will be disqualified.

Stewards : Messrs. F. T. Andrews, T. W. Barnes, A. E. Bennett, J. W. Godsall, F. Lock.

The " W. J. Rimell " SILVER PERPETUAL CHALLENGE CUP (value 100 gns.) For the best sample of Hops in the Show. Open to growers throughout the United Kingdom.

To be competed for by the Prize-winning Samples in Classes 36 to 44.

The "George Bevan" MEMORIAL CUP, for the best sample of Fuggles in the Show, grown in Herefordshire or Worcestershire.

To be competed for annually.

The "E. G. Shew" MEMORIAL ROSEBOWL, for the best sample of Goldings or Golding varieties in the Show, grown in Herefordshire or Worcestershire.

To be competed for annually.

The "John Hill" MEMORIAL CUP, for the best sample of Hops in the Show, grown within the radius of the Society.

To be competed for annually.

A SILVER CHALLENGE SALVER in Class 39 the gift of the Bruff Manufacturing Co., Ltd.

A SILVER CHALLENGE SALVER in Class 38 the gift of Messrs. George Hinds Ltd.

A Pint and a Half-pint TANKARD will be awarded for the first and second best dried and managed hand picked samples respectively (in the opinion of the Judges) shown by a member of the Society, to be given to the driers.

(The gift of Members of the Ledbury Ploughing Society).

A Pint and a Half-pint TANKARD will be awarded for the first and second best dried and managed machine picked samples respectively (in the opinion of the Judges) shown by a member of the Society, to be given to the driers.

(The gift of Members of the Ledbury Ploughing Society).

11

Ledbury Ploughing Society programme from October 1955, with details of the prizes – cups, rose bowls, salvers and tankards – up for grabs for the various hop classes (© Jim Large)

first-ever class for a dwarf hop, First Gold appeared. Tom Nellist has been a member of the Trumpet & District Agricultural Society since 1961, and treasurer 'for a very long time':

The Society was formed in 1944. If you had an excuse to travel in the war you were allowed extra petrol coupons, so farmers used to carry a front wheel of a tractor in the boot with a puncture in it. If they were stopped, they were 'just going to get it mended!' At the time the Home Guard met in a tin shed behind the Trumpet Inn. They were sitting in there with not much to do, so it was decided they should form a hedging society, mostly farmers of course. The Revd Toynbee farmed Munstone Court then, a very rich vicar, and he became president and after two years of hedging they added ploughing as well, and soon after the roots competitions and

Clockwise from top left: A hop sampling winner at the Trumpet; Ploughing Society Members; Men of the Committee; Women of the Committee (© Trumpet & District Agricultural Society)

hops. And it's gone on ever since. But it has changed. In the late sixties, when John Probert [a popular and well-liked Weston Beggard hop grower and Society president] was steward, there were over 200 samples of hops and in recent years this has fallen to under a hundred.

The overall champion, presented with the splendid E. Lewis Silver Tray, is crowned at the last show of the season, the Tenbury Agricultural Society's Autumn Show. The Second World War years and beyond saw a decline in the hop sampling competitions, until their re-establishment in the mid-1960s. John Rawlings, agronomist of Tenbury Wells and long-time stalwart of the show, was one of those who saw its re-emergence:

In the Autumn of 1967, there were five of us – Humphrey Nott, Richard Elliott, Glyn Morgan and John and Edward Hanley – standing in the porch of the former Russell, Baldwin & Bright auctioneers in Tenbury looking at the five hop samples on display. We said we felt sure we

The Edward Lewis Challenge Trophy (© Marsha O'Mahony) and Edward judging hops
(© Clova Perez Corral/ Herefordshire Life Through a Lens)

could do something better than that. And we did. We got in touch and promoted it amongst all the hop growers. Me and Harry Bufton, the show secretary, went around the two counties chasing hop growers for their samples. We became a very successful show in the autumn. At its height, we had 125-plus samples.

The prizes and categories are a snapshot of local hop lineage: the champion sample is awarded the S.J. Adams Memorial Perpetual Challenge Cup, the reserve champion sample the James Nott Memorial, and the Norman Watkins Perpetual Challenge Cup goes to the dryer of the winning sample.

SAMPLING – THE ART AND THE RITUAL

Hop sampling is still important. People taking samples are getting fewer and fewer, it's quite an art. It seems simple, but there are only certain people who can do it. Tom Nellist

The ploughing match competition mirrors the hop merchant's showroom, where the market value of a hop sample is assessed by colour, aroma and general appearance. A sample that contains leaves or stems, or evidence of disease damage, lowers its value and reduces the chances of a good contract with a brewery. 'Drawing a sample' from a pocket of hops cleanly is what the grower desires, and what the judges and buyers like to see. It is done away from prying eyes, to a small audience, the grower, a farmworker or two, who watch in quiet reverence, waiting for the sample to be lifted out cleanly to reveal the mystery or the mistakes of the picking and the kiln. Like reading tea leaves, the sample can reveal so much. Has it been over-cooked, not dried enough? Maybe it needs to return to the kiln? What about the colour? Bright green, or are there brown patches, a sign of late picking? Are there stalks and leaves in it – an anathema to the grower and certainly not what a brewer wants to see. Mervyn Carless has proved his mettle as a sampler time and again. His wirework skills make him the go-to man at the very beginning of the hop lifecycle and he's there again towards the end, as the sampler of choice:

Mervyn Carless sampling hops
(© Mervyn Carless)

Sampling is a trusted job. Getting it right is just experience really. I use a pair of tongs and draw out one square for the grower to look at for valuation, and one goes to the breweries, and another might go to the ploughing matches. Graham Andrews suggested I might be the right sort of chap because I had the experience to do samples and that's how I started. I used to keep all the samples here at one time, spread across the room. I'd have Robert Lane of Bosbury, John Andrews, Peter Davies of Claston, Simon Parker at Munderfield, all up the Teme Valley.

Sampling is a trusted job. Growers would take my advice, and young dryers would ask me "what do you think of these?" It's very much a touchy-feely sort of job. You know when there's damp hops. You open the pocket up and put your hand in and if it is cold you can feel the moisture in there. If it's too wet I will say, "you have to re-dry these" or, "you've got to have a look at these". We've had a few disasters over the years.

Dublin is home to the Guinness museum. Sitting amongst its collection is a tool that may present something of a mystery. The curator's label indicates where and by whom it was used, so we know of its provenance. It does not look mass-produced; perhaps it has been knocked together in a garage work-shop, or maybe it is the work of a blacksmith. It's metal, maybe a little shy of 18-inches long, with a heavy-duty scissor-like effect, sturdy hand-grips at the top, and at the bottom a fork-like clamp. This is the sampler's tool. Like the haulier's handling hooks, or the stringer's monkey, the stilt-man's stilts, this belongs to the sampler, and him alone. It is an important, if not modest, part of the hop story, because sampling is, at its essence, all about showing one's wares to potential buyers, and it has to look good. And a tool is only as good as the man or woman using it.

Drawing a traditional grading sample from a pocket or a bale requires a methodical approach. First, the sampler uses a sharp knife to cut the seams of the pocket. Then, using hauling hooks, the seams are pinned back to reveal the compressed contents. Straddling the pocket, the sampler cuts two straight lines in the hops before thrusting in the sampling tool and the hop sample is withdrawn and trimmed to shape, like slicing a loaf of bread. When the grower is satisfied, the sample is wrapped in blue paper, held in place with a brass pin and labelled with the grower's name, variety and crop year. The job is finished when the sampler resews the pocket and returns it to storage, where it will await a sale or collection from the brewer.

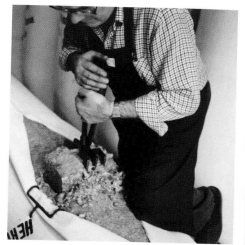

John Burgess using the sampling tool at The Grange, Bosbury (© John Burgess)

The tool once belonged to no-nonsense manager at Guinness Hop Farms at Braces Leigh, Malvern, John Burgess. It ceased operations in the mid-1980s and John was asked by Western Quality Hops (WQH), one of the growers' co-operatives, to be their sampler. It is John's sampling tool that is part of the brewing giant's archive in Dublin today. He and his wife Heather worked as a team; John sampling and Heather wrapping. John is 92:

It was J.F. Brown who put my sampling tool into the Guinness museum. He had an illustrious war record and was awarded the DSO. He was very typical of the sort of old boy network at Guinness. He ended up as their head brewer in Dublin, well, that was like being one next to god. He also wrote *Guinness and Hops,* published by Arthur Guinness in 1980. He eventually retired to Colwall and was interested in the sampling. It was hard work and I was so busy that the growers used to re-stitch the pockets for me. The most important thing was to show the hops at their best, clean cut and packed properly, and the wrapping folded correctly. Your hands would get covered in resin when handling hops, so Heather had to be careful when she was wrapping. You didn't want any stains on the paper. These samples were the showcase of the crop and had to be clean and tidy and neat. Then every night we would take the samples to Jill Andrews at Bosbury, who was secretary of Western Quality Hops.

COMPETITION JUDGING

There's not a great deal of reverential unwrapping of the blue paper to reveal what lies beneath. They come from the hop and brewing industries and know what they are looking for. Cupped hands lift the hops to their noses, the hops are rubbed in their hands, another sniff. Is there an aroma? How much stickiness is there? It's all part of the skill of the judging. Peter Walker

The public is ushered out of the judging area when the judging commences. First, the pin is removed, the paper falls back in such a way as to conceal the grower's name but revealing the precious contents. Initially, the judges just look, what does the sample reveal visually: signs of disease perhaps, extraneous leaves or stalks? There is some pointing, murmurings, conferring and shoulder-shrugging. Then gently they start to pick the samples up, lightly breaking them into two, examining the contents, more sniffing. Now they take a piece of the sample and rub their hands together, cup them and take in the aroma. What is it they smell: is it grassy, honey-like, bitter, spicy? All the senses are employed here. Except taste. That comes later at the bar. Judges discuss, winners are decided and trophies handed over.

Charles Pudge was chief steward of the hop section at the Ledbury Society for 21 years and he made great efforts to organise some of these big players in the industry as judges:

Left: Terry Young wrapping hop samples at the Hop Marketing Board's Ledbury warehouse (© Hop Pocket Museum). *Right*: Hop factor David Samuels with hop samples at the Three Counties Show (© David Powell, Bank Farm, Rochford)

Historically the judge would have been a merchant, a brewer and a factor, someone who had some respect in the hop trade. Over the years we've had judges from Wiggins & Richardson, Walton Bedell, Hestleburgers, Bass or Whitbread, Wolverhampton & Dudley. We even had some come from London and Kent. It was very competitive. I can clearly remember Mr Le May, the hop factor, judging regularly. These competitions were highly regarded in their day.

SILVER ROSE BOWLS, TROPHIES, TRAYS AND TANKARDS: THE HOP PRIZES

Winning growers were offered rich rewards. Past donations of silverware and crystal-ware to all three societies have been given by merchants, the likes of Morris Hanbury and Le May. The Wiggins Richardson trophy first presented as a winning prize nearly 60 years ago, stands over two feet tall, and is made of solid silver. Such silverware was a measure of the prestige these competitions once commanded. Ray Morris has won the Rimmell cup at the Ledbury match and it would horrify the Society to learn where it was stored: 'I had to get them insured, they were worth a lot of money. I hid them under the bed!'

There are other hop competitions besides those held at Tenbury, Ledbury and Trumpet Agricultural Societies. Mark Andrews of Townend Farm, Bosbury, competes at local and national levels. His early hop-growing career was at Pomona Farm, Bartestree, before going on to manage the Allied Breweries

Farm at Brierley Court in the 1990s. Peter Davies of Claston and Dormington was an early influence on his career. In 2020, Mark's Harlequin Hop was crowned Overall Champion at Britain's National Hop competition for the second year running. This competition, run by the Institute of Brewing and Distilling, dates back to 1944 and is judged by a panel of Master Brewers. Mark was also awarded Supreme Champion at the Charles Faram Well-Hopped World Series Awards in 2019. He still sends his hop samples to the local competitions:

> It's nice to have a bit of a banter, bit of competition and quite nice to win a prize. I'm a member of the Ledbury Ploughing Society, but I put samples in all three shows and have won the Edward Lewis silver platter quite a few times. It helps because the brewers just keep an eye on these sorts of things and it just puts your name out there, helps your cause when it comes to selling.

Clockwise from top left: Ray Morris (second left) and his team at Burton Mill, hop winners at the Tenbury Show. Ned Watkins (first left) was Ray's dryer (© Ray Morris); Graham and Barbara Andrews with a winning cup at The Grange (© Andrews family); the Thompson family at Little Lambswick celebrate their clean sweep at the Tenbury Show (© Roger Brace)

8

Selling the hop

Crops could not be forecasted with much hope of accuracy. Hops were the most uncertain of all, and there was highly organised betting on the likely yield of the hop excise duty; members of Tattersall's indulged and there was an annual Hop Settling Dinner at a Worcester inn, with a croupier presiding to settle heavy bets, most of which had been hopefully misplaced owing to frequent last-minute changes in the condition of the crop and the weather for picking.

E.L. Jones, *Season & Prices:*
The role of weather in English Agricultural History, 1964

THE GOLDEN AGE

THE nineteenth century was the Golden Age for the hop industry, with hop acreage reaching a peak of 77,000 in 1878. A hopyard would have been a far more familiar sight then, known to all, and a source of employment for many. However, that changed as beer drinkers' palates developed a taste for lighter beers, the Indian Ales and Pale Ales. By 1909 only 32,000 acres of land were devoted to hops. This, coupled with a renewed import of foreign hops, led to an industry struggling. Today, selling the English hop in an aggressive and competitive global market is one of the most significant challenges facing the UK industry. Marketing hops is a very different discipline to growing them, as veteran grower Graham Andrews once remarked: 'It took me 20 years of farming on my own to learn how to grow hops and I'm sure it took me another 30 years to learn how to sell them properly. It's one thing producing them. It's another thing altogether getting them sold.'

The first delivery of hops to Worcester after the Second World War
(© Philip Bowler, Frome Valley Transport)

Green sacks and a pocket of hops at Much Cowarne, Herefordshire (© Neil Wright)

HOP MARKETS

Hop trading has been part of the fabric of Worcester city centre since the 1730s. The fine redbrick building on Foregate Street, was the focus of hop trading for the Midlands and beyond up until the early 1900s. Its flamboyant structure and gilt lettering signalled one thing: the profitability and importance of hops to the commercial life of the county. It was the centre of hop trading, and transactions could get unruly. In September 1901, the *Worcester Advertiser* reported on, 'Disorderly scenes at Worcester hop market'. The growers were not happy and had mobbed the buyers because 'the crop was too plentiful, and we are unhappy at the price we are being given'. The day presented a scene of unprecedented disorder, which almost deserved to be called a riot!

Hereford growers considered themselves the poor relations when it came to hop markets. In the nineteenth century they were yet to have their own market and it was a sore point for many. There were reasons for this. Infrastructure was a problem for this isolated county. The River Wye had been used to transport hops, but as a trading route it was beset with scheduling problems: it relied on water levels and was dictated, therefore, by the seasons. The best hope for opening up Herefordshire hops to a broader market was the railway. A letter to the *Hereford Times* in 1847 urged action:

Whenever we have a railway into this city, immediate steps must be taken for establishing a hop market here, in order that the farmers may dispose of Hereford hops in their own county, and not have the trouble of journeying to a distant market to sell what may be disposed of at their own doors – great parts of the hops of Herefordshire being disposed of at Worcester, acquire the title 'Worcester hops' and thus robs us of the celebrity of our own county's growth.

After many promises and false starts, the railway eventually puffed into the county in 1853, and by 1857 the Corn Exchange was built in Broad Street, home also to the city's hop market. It eventually closed in 1950, leaving a waft of memories. In a postcard home in the 1920s, a visiting Welsh miner described the 'sour smell of hops' as he walked along Broad Street. A few years later a young woman was raising her nose heavenwards, 'giving an ecstatic *ahhhh*, and sniffing the air with as much appreciation as Bisto kids.' Others, however, exclaimed 'yuck, clutching our noses, we hurried on as quickly as possible.'

THE BOROUGH – CENTRE OF HOP BUYING AND SELLING

After 1750 and until the Second World War, hop factors and hop merchants in The Borough increasingly took on the sale and purchase of hops. The selling of hops by factors on behalf of growers to merchants, acting for brewers, gradually became the predominant method of marketing and the respective middleman functions continued with little change under the management of the Hop Marketing Board from 1932 to 1982. Celia Cordle, *Out of the Hay and into the Hops*, 2011

In the 1890s the telephone exchange call-word for The Borough district was simply 'Hop'. This area of Southwark was unquestionably the heart of UK hop selling. It was a place of handshakes, deals, negotiations, arguments, secretiveness, money made and money lost. Come autumn-time and post-harvest, growers converged on this Thames-side district, their best suits on, ties tight around the collar. There are still traces of the old trading place at Borough today. The hop warehouses were fine redbrick buildings, built with flourish and hop money, the names of hop factors chiselled high up for all to see, painted in gilt. It was an era and a place that suggested old-style gentlemanly trading, Homburg Hats and pocket watches.

The hop factors and hop merchants were the middle men, the buyers and sellers. Even after the formation of the Hop Marketing Board in 1932, hop factors continued as dual agents for the Board and individual growers. Most often they were family businesses, and gentlemen, most of the time: Le May, Samuels, Wigan Richardson, Hesselberger and Gaskain, J.H. Matthews & Co. to name but a few; knowledgeable, often kindly, occasionally neglectful, they undertook the grading, valuation, centralised storage and marketing of hops. Growers had one or even two factors – 'We were hedging our bets' rationalised one grower. The factor's mastery was in the grading of samples, the quality and the pureness of the hops. The factor didn't want to see stalks or leaves. Different grades attracted different prices, and a good sale at a high price led to a higher commission.

The hop factor was an aesthete and a charming one too; 'They would take your money off you, give you lunch once a year, chat you up, then go away again,' mused Edward Lewis. Nevertheless, they had their commission to look after and wanted the best for their growers. They pulled out all the stops for the growers' annual visit to the capital and visits to their showrooms. Peter Walker:

We used to have jollies up to London in December, when the samples were shown. They selected our samples and we went to see how they looked and to have feedback on what we could have done differently, because they could tell from the samples how much disease was in them, whether we had dried them too fast or too slowly. All these things would come from their expertise.

But a lot of farmers were actually in hock to their factors and merchants; the factors were acting as their bankers. Basically, in order to get the harvest in, you needed the money in advance, which is why the factor had an interest in getting it right. In July or August, they would come around the farms to see how you were doing. They were advisors really. And of course, they would give you the local gossip, "up the valley they've got a problem with the red spider, so you better watch out for that", and "we'll have a good look and see if we can find any", things like that. They were city gents mostly. I remember at Christmas time they would send a bottle of whisky, or a bottle of sherry and 200 cigarettes for Mother, Senior Service always.

Graham Andrews (*right*) of The Grange, Bosbury, with Barry Moore (*left*), a buyer for Bass Breweries, and Michael Wigan (*middle*), one of the owners at Wigan Richardson, a hop merchant business (© Andrews family)

The irony of these gifts was not lost on their clients. John Pudge: 'The strange thing about the hop factor was that we paid them out of our money and they would send things like cheeses and boxes of apples in December. And of course, it was coming out of our money anyway! Took it out of their commission.'

John Pudge's father and grandfather once overheard two hop factors on one of their trips to The Borough:

> Dad and Pop were on a train going somewhere across London along the Thames and were listening in on a couple of hop merchants who were talking about how rough the crop was that year. They said there was a number of samples that should be chucked in the river because they were not so good. Now, because Dad and Pop always prided themselves on having good quality crops, Dad turned around to Pop and said, "I think some of ours should have been chucked in there as well!"

Direct buying and selling between the grower and the brewer was considered ungentlemanly and was frowned upon, and efforts to keep the grower and brewer apart sometimes verged on the farcical. Edward Lewis:

> The factor and the merchant would talk to each other but they would not let the farmer and the brewer near each other. We used to market half ours with Le May and the other half with Wild & Gaskain. So you'd go to one and let them look at your samples, and then you'd go around the corner to the other one and say you'd left your hat behind with the first.

The Eveson Trust

In October 1993 a Herefordshire-born woman left an estate worth £49 million in her will. This was the personal fortune of a Bishops Frome native, Violet Mary Eveson. The Eveson Charitable Trust was set up to distribute the income from her estate, which it continues to do today, funding projects across the region. Violet was the only grandchild of William Farmer Pudge of Upper House, Bishops Frome. He was born at New House in 1851 and built up such a large hop-growing empire during the latter part of the nineteenth century that he was at one time said to be the largest private grower in the UK and the biggest hop-growing business in Europe. His series of kilns, running side-by-side, were ahead of their time. He travelled around the Midlands and Manchester and further north with a special hop suitcase con-

W.F. Pudge's huge range of hop kilns at Bishops Frome (© Edward Lewis)

taining his hop samples, big cubes, larger than the contemporary ones, that fitted neatly inside. On visits to various breweries, he undid the locks, and flipped the suitcase lid open, like the consummate salesman, revealing the pungent contents. Indeed, pockets of hops sold to Black Country breweries became known as 'Pudges'. Violet married at Bishops Frome Church and it was said that a red carpet ran from her family home to the church, and afterwards the wedding reception took place in the empty kiln buildings, decorated for the occasion. Many of the guests at the wedding came from the hop-growing world. Violet inherited the family's farming and financial empire, controlling it from her home in Stourbridge, which her grandfather had built for her as a wedding present in 1928. The beneficiaries of the Eveson Trust Fund continue to do good work for West Midlands communities into the twenty-first century.

Left: Bill Le May, hop factor, Richard Rayner and Dr George Howard judging hop classes (© Trumpet & District Agricultural society). *Above*: Hop factor invoice for J.H. Matthews (© HARC)

And when you got to the other one, you'd say you'd left your coat behind!

The factors would take their samples and that's what they sold your crop on and put them on display and the brewers would come around. You either went to see what the brewer had bought or what they were going to buy. Then the factor would say to the farmer, "well this is why we couldn't get a good price Mr Lewis", and then say to the brewer, "these are bloody marvellous aren't they!" It was a good day out mostly.

For some, trips to The Borough were an opportunity to go out and enjoy a spot of drinking. Brian Willder:

They knew their clients; they knew the ones that were serious drinkers and wanted a good time, and they knew the ones who were serious about the business in hand. So the serious drinkers were plied with gin from the moment they stepped through the door until they put them on the train to send them home in the evening.

Some hop factors were benign and kindly businessmen; others were less so. Stafford Le May mentored a young Brian Willder, who had managed a hop farm in Hampshire:

A good relationship with your hop factor was important. When I was starting out my factor was Stafford Le May who looked after our hops and he took me under his wing and showed me what good hops looked like. It was very kind of him and he used to give me a ten-shilling note at the end. They were really nice gentlemen, knew their business, their clients and their hops well. He was interested in what I was doing and was very encouraging. And when we went to The Borough he'd take me off and show me where things had gone wrong and where things were very right. And he also used to show me other people's hops, so we could have a comparison, "see, this is what really good hops look like". He was a sort of mentor.

Brian arrived to a new position managing hopyards at Leighton Court in 1978. There he discovered a yard not in the best of conditions. It was dilapidated, the wirework was rusting and the yard full of weeds. One of the first jobs was to meet the factor, but not Mr Le May. It was an eye-opening afternoon as Brian slowly learned of the wretched state of the hopyard. A lot of work lay ahead:

It was so embarrassing. This factor was telling us what lovely hops these were. There were some hops, but I tried not to look at the hawthorn bush growing up beside it. I couldn't believe what he was saying and how everything was in such wonderful condition. So the following spring, just as the growth was starting, he came back with a sidekick. I wasn't so keen on meeting them, but I knew I had to. After a preliminary hand-shake he said, "I hope you are going to continue letting us factoring your hops?" I thought for a moment and said, "actually no. What I want from my hop factor is to tell me the truth. This client wants the truth and nothing but the truth!"

Buildings at The Borough suffered bomb damage during the Blitz campaign of the Second World War and this hastened the end of several hundred years of hop trading in the area, and by the early 1950s the Hop Marketing Board, under whose auspice's factors traded, moved to Paddock Wood in Kent, a journey too far for some. The annual pilgrimage to The Borough had had its day.

Hauling the hops – a work of art

A pocketful of pressed hops is an unyielding item in a hopyard. They are dead-weight heavy, hard as concrete, with no give at all. 'Ears' and 'toggles' at each of the four corners give the handler some purchase, but not much. Growers and haulage contractors therefore have their cherished hooks to hand at all times. These, and brute strength, are what it takes to load a flat-bed truck with a load of hop pockets. A hop pocket weighs around a hundred-weight and a half (roughly 75 kilos). Hauling these onto the back of his truck, with neither rope nor pulley, was hard, hot, sweaty, tiring work. The pockets had to sit securely and safely. Retired haulier, John Griffiths of Suckley, hauled for many growers in the district.

For John, an 'eye for the job' was equally important. It was not just a matter of lining the pockets up to sit and balance well, but to look impressive. Such aesthetics were not just for his benefit, but for the grower's too: they looked good on the back of the truck as they travelled to the next stage of their journey, the hop warehouses. It is still a source of great pride to him decades later:

> We took them all over the country, to warehouses – Farams had three in Worcester, Pudges at Bishops Frome stored a huge amount and went straight to breweries at Shepton Mallet and Burton-on-Trent. Dad hauled hops before me and I remember back in 1946, I was about ten, helping him load them, getting in the way, muddy boots walking over the hop pockets. He wasn't happy about that.
>
> We were one of the biggest hop hauliers around here. I took pride putting my pockets on. It was a job for young, fit men. You were standing 14-feet off the ground and your balance had to be good and you needed a strong back. You had a great old hook and you wrapped the rope, you didn't tie any knots. You use a looping system, which has been tried and tested on timber-hauling for hundreds of years I should think. In all the years I was loading hops, I never had a load slip.

Top: A flat-bed truck laden with pockets (© John Griffiths). *Above left*: Derek Gwynne with a lorry-load of pockets (from Guinness farms at Braces Leigh, near Malvern) at Bristol Docks, bound for Dublin by boat (© Suzanne Gwynne). *Above right*: Frome Valley Transport truck in 1962 at Munderfield, driven by Hubert 'Buck' George Pullen (© Pullen/ Chedgzoy/ Mowbray families)

A lorry-load of hop pockets, c.1940s (© Brian Willder)

THE HOP MARKETING BOARD

Heavy crops in 1929 and 1930, with no marketing control, forced the price of hops down to a very low level; a light crop in 1931 raised the price slightly, but it was still below the cost of production. These three years of loss strained the financial resources of many hop growers; some were forced out of the industry, and many others reduced their acreage of hops. A.H. Burgess, *Hops: Botany, Cultivation and Utilization*, 1964

The crisis of the industry in the late 1920s called for some form of marketing control to ensure the survival of the industry. And so, in 1932, with just 16,500 acres of hops left in the UK, the Hop Marketing Board (HMB) was formed. It brought some stability to the industry, but it was not the panacea many hoped it would be. The HMB negotiated a guaranteed price with the growers, and the brewers indicated their expected demand to the Board, resulting in an allocated quota system. The scheme was successful in ensuring growers and brewers were protected from the violent price fluctuations of earlier years. Others, however, worried that the HMB dampened entrepreneurial spirit, being averse to risk. Some growers believe the UK market is still recovering from the effects of the HMB today.

The transition period from controlled market to an open one proved challenging for some businesses and individuals. Old habits were hard to shed for Jim Colston, who was MD at hop merchants Charles Faram & Co. Ltd for much of the duration of the HMB. Current MD Paul Corbett arrived in 1989 and describes his senior colleague as very good around the technical side of hops, but less so around selling:

> Jim had been used to working under the HMB when everything operated under a quota system. For example, he would go to Bass in Burton, announce himself at reception and he was told to take a seat. Within ten minutes a butler, in full butler regalia, including white gloves, would come down the sweeping staircase, with lovely carpet and brass rods across, carrying a silver tray with an envelope on. He would offer the tray to Jim, who would take the envelope and put it in his top pocket without even reading it – he knew that that was his order for that year because it had already been agreed by the quota! Ten minutes later all the brewers would come down and all go off to the pub. Not a word was exchanged.

The Hop Marketing Board building in Ledbury, with hop haulier delivering hops, in 1965
(© Derek Evans/ HARC)

Of course, Jim being used to that way of doing business, when the HMB was eventually disbanded, he really didn't have that sales and marketing expertise to take the business forward. Quite often I would be sat there, and Jim would get his lunch out on a nice big white plate, with a knife and fork, and sit at his table and tuck his handkerchief in the top of his tie and sit there and polish off his prawn salad, and ten or fifteen minutes I would hear some snoring! John Farbon, the MD before me, used to come back from travelling to visit breweries and would ask Jim, "called anyone this afternoon?" "No." "Has anyone called you?" "No." That's the way it used to be done. Jim had no idea how to generate business in the competitive world. There were no demands under the HMB to chase orders.

But he was very good technically on the hop side of things and was very good with the grading and the assessment of hops. He taught me a lot and gave me a very good grounding in the quality of the hops. But in terms of sales training, it was non-existent really.

In 1982, as the UK entered the Common Market, the HMB was wound up because its monopolistic structure was seen to violate EU rules. In its place, five producer-led co-operatives emerged, creating a new marketing group for a new generation of growers with a common aim: selling hops and creating a national and a global brand. Today, the surviving grower co-operatives are English Hops Ltd, Hawkbrand Hops Ltd and Wealden Hops Ltd. All are members of the British Hop Association, formed by British growers in 1996.

GROWER CO-OPERATIVES

The co-operatives' members come from all the hop-growing areas of the UK, plus a few more from the Continent's hop-growing regions. Healthily competitive, they all experience the peaks and troughs of an industry that never allows a grower to rest on his or her laurels. Richard Phillips of Lower Eggleton Court is the model of the twentieth-century hop grower. Chairman of English Hops Ltd, he acts on behalf of the other member growers, marketing their hops, both here and overseas, and particularly in the States, where the potential market is enormous:

> I market on behalf of the growers, so we sell to some of the hop merchants, like Charles Faram and Steiner's, they are our two main customers. Hop factor would be the old-fashioned word for me; I am the liaison between the grower and the purchaser. I always try to do my very best for the growers to make sure they get as good a return as possible. We do quite a bit of PR with different breweries and I travel out to America every year to go to the craft brewer's convention, which attracts about ten or twelve thousand people associated with the brewing industry. I'll be there with Charles Faram helping to promote British hops to American brewers.

Simon Parker, a director of Hawkbrand Hops, says change has had to happen for the industry to thrive:

> There are 2,000 breweries at the moment and a lot of them use foreign hops. They don't want to make beer that is like traditional beer, like other brewers; they want a different flavour profile, so they try a different profile hop from abroad to make their beer with. And on the back of that we have been exporting hops for the same reason. Our producer group, Hawkbrand, was set up by another hop grower, Thomas Hawkins. He went on to buy the Charles Faram business. That's been good for West

Midlands hop growers and those in the south east as well. All our hops go through Farams, and we still have that exclusive relationship today. Like most crops, you wouldn't want to be growing it without a contract, and you basically secure your contract before you grow the crop. And we have that with Farams. Through them we've exported some of our Pilgrim hops to the New Belgium Brewery in Chicago for example.

THE MERCHANT

Your hop merchant: friend or foe? Modern merchants represent a combination of hard-working commodity dealers – the commodity increasingly alpha acid – and industrialists. For their living they rely entirely not only on their customers the brewers, but equally on their suppliers, the growers. Without these they would be out of business. It follows that they have every incentive to ensure the survival of a happy hop-growing industry and to behave as the hop grower's friend, not foe! Ralph Kenber, MD of hop merchants Lupofresh, speaking at the Economic Committee of the International Hop Growers' Convention, Strasbourg, 1983 The eponymous Charles Faram was born into the trade. He was born in his father's pub in north London. By 1865 he had set up as hop merchant in Worcester's Foregate Street, close to the city's hop market, during the industry's golden age. Starting from a small office, he rented a hop storehouse in nearby Southfield Street. Today, over 150 years later, the Charles Faram name continues as a merchant of hops and hop products, and a one-stop-shop for the brewing industry. Other merchants include Steiners and Lupofresh. At Charles Faram there are industry veterans at the helm. Technical Director Will Rogers is from a hop background; his father Henry is a former grower at Weston Beggard.

Just like the old days at The Borough, grading of samples is still an important part of the buying process, this time at Faram's HQ in Malvern. Will:

We're almost going back to the original route of factoring and merchanting and we work closely with growers. We purchase a lot of hops in the USA and have offices in Toronto, Portland Oregon and Yakima. So we buy and sell hops within those markets as well, and within Europe we buy German, Polish, Slovenian and Czech hops. And we will sell those back into those markets as well as bring them into the UK. After the harvest, the marketing companies, Hawkbrand, English Hops, Wealden or Western Quality Hops, will send us samples to represent our contracts, and they will have graded the samples. One is the grower's sample and one is the merchant's sample. They should be cut from the same bale or pocket. We will have a look and see if there are any signs of disease and will give them a grade.

Paul Corbett, Charles Faram's MD, and I then go through all the samples and either agree or disagree on the grading of the sample. This really comes down to experience, years in the game. There will be hundreds of samples each time and we have to be pretty quick. The grower doesn't want to wait too long to hear if their hops are of acceptable quality or not. You become quite adept at it. We lay the samples out and you can even tell, just by looking at them, if they have been picked on a wet day, just by looking at them.

The lead-in between the introduction of a new variety and it arriving in a pint of beer can be up to a decade. Farams take a long view, studying trends at a global level. This informs their breeding programme. Will again:

It is all about expanding the marketability of UK hops. Consumers are well aware of hop varieties, not just brewers, and they are seeking out the hop varieties in the beers they are drinking. And I don't think that is a trend that's going to go away. There will be a market for big citrusy, tropical fruit characteristics. And we are looking for those from British hops. Ten years ago, we were told it was impossible with our maritime climate to be able to produce those flavours. We think we're just about there. The Harlequin hop is at an advanced farm trial stage and we are very excited about that. In a blind tasting no one even considered it was from the UK and we consider that to be a big success.

The beer market is quite trend driven. At the moment the sales of British hops in the US are a bit slower than we would like and that's why we are developing new varieties. Because some of these are being seen as exotic in the US. They might want tradition, but they might also want exotic. It's trying to appeal to everyone. But certainly, the trend for big hoppy beers has been around for a little while and doesn't appear to be going away soon.

9

Hops to Hostelry: pubs & brewing

I'm an occasional drinker, the kind of guy who goes out for a beer and wakes up in Singapore with a full beard.

Raymond Chandler, *Spanish Blood: a collection of short stories,* 1946

ENGLISH artist William Hogarth captured the joviality and licentiousness of beer in his famous 1751 print, *Beer Street*. This spirit continues, for the most part, in English beer and the traditional pub. Whether it is back-street, high street, village green, lonely outpost, salubrious or scruffy, it is embedded in British culture, as familiar as fish'n' chips, and scones and clotted cream. Step inside these community spaces, and you are immediately hit with the familiar and comforting smell of beer. It overrides everything else. It has become part of the fabric of the building, impregnating the wood, the walls. From the outside, you step in, onto a quarry-tiled floor perhaps, brick fireplace in front if you are lucky, bare-oak seating or maybe the odd cushioned one, wooden tables or even Formica-topped, beer mats scattered. Focus of attention is the bar, lit from above, shelves and bottles out of reach behind, overhead hang glasses. Drip-trays and towelling cloths jostle for space on the bar top. Immediately in front, lined up like orderly skittles, are the beer

(© Gonzalo Remy, Unsplash)

219

pumps with their contents displayed on wildly inventive pump clip art: The Hop Father, Swan on the Wye, Talbot Blonde, Phoenix, Frizzle, Kingstone Gold, Ledbury Pale Ale or Welder. Maybe you are looking for an old familiar beer, or something new. With a few sharp pulls on the pump, your pint glass is filled, foam floating lightly on top, the glass is passed across the bar. It promises so much: light, dancing freshness, sprightly, zesty, honey-like sweetness, bittersweet, exuberance, quaffability, all flavours and mannerisms of the English hopped beer. Each pleasing slurp contains within it the story of the hop, connecting twenty-first-century beer drinkers to lands and histories that have been forgotten in an era of industrial food production.

The barrel store at the Watkins Brewery in Hereford, taken by Alfred Watkins early in the twentieth century (© Herefordshire Libraries)

HOPS IN ENGLISH BEER

Undoubtedly, the main function of hops in brewing is to bitter beer, but increased quantities are being employed for imparting hop character. Hop Marketing Board magazine, March 1983

The first record of hopped beer in England was for a batch imported from Amsterdam in 1362, and the earliest mention of beer brewed in England from imported hops was in 1412, made by a German alewife in Colchester. Hops were a relatively late addition to beer, most likely popularised by these ale women, whose cottage industries brewed recipes over ranges or open fires. An entry in the Domesday Book for Hereford suggested brewing was done only by wives. The addition of hops to their brews, with their natural antiseptic and preservative qualities, provided households with a safe alternative to drinking water. This new concoction was, in many respects, a life-saver and has remained the foundation stone of the English beer tradition, a pleasing, comforting, thirst-quenching bitterness.

Ale and beer are interchangeable terms today, but it wasn't always that way. Their recipes were very different. Ale was made with malted barley, flavoured with herbs and spices, the likes of bog myrtle, yarrow, meadow sweet and rosemary, but no hops. Beer was another malted barley drink but lighter, this time thanks to the addition of hops.

Roger Putman is a Master Brewer, a committee member of the Brewing History Society and editor for the Institute of Brewing's magazine. He served his time as brewer for 30 years with Bass, producing beer and lager. He is an expert in brewing processes, both macro and micro brews, and is committed to standards of excellence in our brewing industries. What is the relevance of hops today?

Hops are there to balance flavours and have a pleasant aroma. They are added later in the brewing process so that beers, particularly English golden ales, smell nice and hoppy. It's worth noting that the brewing industry kind of nurtured the industrial revolution in this country, in refreshing workers that were working hard for a living. There was a big tradition of pub-going then and a big tradition of brewing to support it. Until about 1750, there were no big brewers at all, an ale woman perhaps, a farm house, a cottage industry. Then the common brewers as they were known, the wholesale brewers, set up and started to supply pubs more remotely, and indeed to export beer to the colonies. Burton Pale Ale even went to India and had to be fairly robust to stand the journey of several months. It most certainly contained hops from the West Midlands.

Burtonisation

Why, if 'tis dancing you would be,
There's brisker pipes than poetry.
Say, for what were hopyards meant,
Or why was Burton built on Trent?
Oh many a peer of England brews
Livelier liquor than the Muse,
And malt does more than Milton can
To justify God's ways to man.
Ale, man, ale's the stuff to drink

A.E. Housman, A Shropshire Lad LXII (1896)

Burton on Trent's brewing fame was such that in 1896 A.E. Housman mentioned it in his famous poem, A Shropshire Lad. This town owes its brewing pedigree to its famous, hard well-water. Containing high levels of calcium sulphate and bicarbonates, it is perfect for beers that highlight the hop character such as Bitter and India Pale Ale. Most brewers, however, do not have access to well-water like Burton's. Instead they rely on the local mains water, known in brewing parlance as 'town liquor'. But they can emulate the Burton water effect in their brewing, through a process known as Burtonisation, which, in simplest terms, means adding mineral salts to the water. By the late nineteenth century, one quarter of all beer sold in the UK was brewed in Burton. Aside from its magical well-water, hops from Herefordshire, Shropshire and Worcestershire were on the list of ingredients.

THE EMPIRE AND ENGLISH PALE ALE

As the Empire expanded, wooden ships sailed from the English coast carrying beer either as an alternative to water, for daily rations to keep the crew content, as ballast, or even as a trading commodity. From the founding of the East India Company in 1600, the first English settlement in Virginia in 1607, Australia's penal colony in Botany Bay in 1788, British ships carried beer across the globe. Burton India Pale was a beer success story. Bright and clear, refreshing for the climate, robust, high in alcohol and highly hopped; it must have been a welcome sight to expats all over. But they were soon demanding it back home too. In 1827 a ship carrying a consignment of Burton India Pale Ale was wrecked in the Irish Sea soon after leaving for the Indian sub-continent. Fortunately, several casks were salvaged and later sold in Liverpool by insurance underwriters. Such was the reaction to this new beer, that very soon people were clamouring for this 'export' beer across Britain. When the railway reached Burton in 1839, a Burton Pale Ale craze swept the nation.

MACROBREWERIES – THE BIG PLAYERS

The rich hop-growing ground in the area has attracted big players from the brewing world, Allied Breweries and Guinness Hop Farms among them. By 1886, Guinness was the largest brewer in the world, with an annual output of 1.2 million barrels. Guinness Hop Farms Ltd arrived in the region in 1946, establishing a huge operation at Braces Leigh, Malvern, continuing the successes of sister farms Udiam and Bodium in Kent. The combined annual harvest of all three provided enough hops to supply Guinness Breweries with three month's supply. And not just for its Park Royal or Dublin brewing sites, but its other bases too, from Lagos in Nigeria to Tokyo in Japan. John Burgess was the last manager at Braces Leigh before Guinness Hop Farms closed in 1987 after nearly 40 years of hop growing there. He knew what they wanted from him and the hopyard, having spent several years already at Bodium. At Braces Leigh he instilled a military-like behaviour at picking time. John:

> Our last crop was in 1987 and we harvested 280 acres of hops, mostly Bullion, some Challenger. We picked and dried it in 20 days turning out a hundred bales a day. They were then loaded in the afternoon when the haulage contractor arrived, went straight to the port, and they were at

Herefordshire victuallers and MP David Gibson-Watt in Westminster (*above*) and visiting the Guinness Brewery sites (all © John Ridgway)

Dublin brewery the next morning ready for brewing. Our brewers wanted the alphas [alpha acids from hops contribute to the bitterness in beer]. It was very important; it was all Guinness wanted. People talk about clean and dirty pickers and Guinness got blamed for a lot. But Guinness is dark black stuff. If it had a leaf in it, then that leaf had alpha on it too. Of course, they didn't want it too dirty a sample because of the logistics of it and the added weight that might bring.

I had a good relationship with the hop department at Guinness Brewery in Dublin. I was sometimes flown over there in the Guinness plane for meetings. It was an opportunity to see where the hops were going and meet the men in the brewery, who would give us advice on hops, "you ought to do this or that", this sort of thing. It was all useful information.

Working alongside John was another no-nonsense character, Charlie Morris. Charlie, 80, was born in Hatfield near Puddleston during the war, and didn't see a picking machine until 1965 when he was a bailiff at Garford Farm:

It was a hop farm and the first hop machine I saw was when I was 23. I was thrown in the deep end but coped very well. I was there 17 years until I was made redundant and then came to Guinness Hop Farms. I learnt a lot by watching and remembering and seeing how people did things. Mother used to take me hop picking when I was ten and make me pick the leaves out. I thought I never wanted to see another hop again. I thought it was a bloody terrible job.

But then I started at Braces Leigh and there were 280 acres of wirework by the time we finished there. I put up 35 acres in my time. We had a sister farm in Kent and we used to liaise with it. When I first arrived at Braces Leigh, we had three hop-picking machines that had been improved by Guinness, basically Bruff machines that had been adapted with belts and pickers on the front of it. We were growing a lot of Bullion, Challenger and Northdown. Bullion was a robust crop, a lot of people couldn't manage it, it would block the machine up and wouldn't be that clean, but Guinness weren't that bothered about that. They brewed beer with whatever you sent. But there was always this thing that you had your hops nice and clean, no bits in them, and I was brought up to be a clean picker. I had that discipline in me.

Guinness would have been one of the first to put dried hops into bales. It was easier to get them over to Ireland that way. They were all picked up by a hoist and put on a lorry that used to come every day. I know I couldn't get the bales more than 15-foot high otherwise they couldn't get them on the ferry, they would have been too high. We would have liked to put another layer on sometimes to get rid of them, but they just didn't fit.

We used to go down to the brewery in London quite regular, Park
Royal. It was a trip for workmen going down there, have a meal and a
look around. Just a jolly really, see where the hops were going. We used to
go around the brewery, but I never want to go around again because all
you look at is pipes! We would have several glasses of Guinness before we
went on the bus. Pissed when we came from there, I can tell you that!

CHEERS TO GORDON BROWN!

The number of UK pubs and bars increased in 2019 by 315. This modest
resurgence highlighted a return to growth for smaller pubs and bars – many
attached to microbreweries – for the first time in 15 years. It was cheering
news after many years of domination from the brewing giants (including
Diagio, Heineken and Budweiser). And it was largely down to the former
Chancellor of the Exchequer and Labour MP, Gordon Brown. In 2002, in
an increasingly competitive market, he gave small breweries a boost by introducing a progressive beer duty and cutting taxes by 50% on the first 500,000
litres produced every year. But it was only for breweries producing less than
3 million litres total per year. It meant that small brewers could keep prices
low and compete with larger breweries.

There are a healthy number of breweries right across the West Midlands,
including Hobsons, Kingstone Brewery, Spilsbury & Jones Brewing Co.,
Ledbury Real Ales, Swan Brewery, The Hop Shed, The Monkey Shed, The
Tap House, The Three Tuns Brewery, Bewdley Brewery, Weobley Brewery,
Wobbly Brewery and Wye Valley Brewery. Vernon Amor is Managing
Director at Wye Valley Brewery. He follows in the footsteps of his father,
Peter, who set the brewery up in 1985. The Barrels, a Wye Valley pub, epitomises their brand, an unapologetic boozer with a clientele that embraces
all ages, groups and genders, regular music and quiz nights, zero pub grub
apart from packets of crisps and peanuts behind the bar. The focus is on
conversation, conviviality and beer. Vernon:

The Barrels is an eighteenth-century coaching inn and is one of the
last multi-roomed pubs in Hereford. It's a down-to-earth drinking
establishment and was home to our brewery for many years. It attracts
an eclectic clientele, who come for the lively, friendly atmosphere and, of
course, excellent beer.

We try to get as many hops as we can locally. In a normal year 75% of the hops we use in our beer grow within a ten-mile radius. Local is really important to us. We know loads of the growers and try to visit them once or twice a year to build on those relationships. We need them to keep growing their hops. We can't make our beer exactly the same way without their specific ingredients.

We're a modern brewery but like to hark back to a traditional process. Fundamentally, our process for brewing beer is centuries-old and we wanted to continue that by using whole hops. It was more of a heart decision than a financial one. Using whole hops is part of the story of making beer and for us provenance is important, and sustainability too.

Brewers tend to classify hops in two ways: first what we call bittering hops, the alpha hops that we boil primarily for the bitterness, and secondly, hops which we select for their aroma characteristics. Traditional English hops don't have that strong citrusy character. They are much subtler. Aroma is the number one deciding factor, and number two are the alpha acids, the bittering compounds. So a classic English hop like Goldings smells a bit honey-like, slightly earthy in a nice way; or a Fuggles can be ever so slightly grassy or spicy. Characteristics of English hops tend to suit British ales which are traditionally a little bit fuller-bodied, more sweetness to them, what brewers call the "mouth feel of the beer", which is how full-bodied it feels.

Gareth Bateman, head brewer at Wye Valley Brewery (© M. O'Mahony); Gill Bullock and Jimmy Swan at Swan Brewery (© Swan Brewery); Richard Philips at The Monkey Shed (© M. O'Mahony)

The problem with industrial scale production is it becomes the lowest common denominator on price. You end up with accountants running very large businesses and they're using the cheapest ingredients. Whereas, if you've got a microbrewery they care about their ingredients and that's really good for hop growers because it means they really care about not just the variety but also volume and quality of the hop going into their beer. Ali Capper, Chair of Wye Hops and Director of the British Hop Association

Small-town breweries were once very much part of the commercial land-scape, using crops from hopyards that were sometimes within a stone's throw of their copper brewing kettle. But there were dangers, and it was not from the consumption of beer, but from submersion in it. In January 1903, the *Ross Gazette* reported on the sad case of Thomas Nichols, assistant brewer at Parker's Brewery: 'He was employed in placing hops into a pan of boiling water and apparently lost his footing and fell in. No one was near at the time, and when the poor fellow was discovered, his life was extinct'.

The microbrewery phenomenon has been broadly welcomed by growers, albeit with a cautionary note: it is not a panacea for the industry. Big con-tracts from the big players are still needed. Nevertheless, we have a stalwart of British comedy to thank for kick-starting the movement in Herefordshire. Herefordshire's CAMRA (Campaign for Real Ale) cite Monty Python's Terry Jones as the person behind the microbrewing revolution. It started in the small market town of Kington in 1977. Hereford CAMRA's *Hopvine* explained:

> The British brewing industry was in decline then with very little
> real ale available; the six giant national brewers were closing down
> regional breweries and opting for keg beer, in the remorseless pursuit
> of profit, taking over and closing many of the remaining independent
> breweries. But Terry Jones was an enthusiastic ale drinker and member
> of CAMRA. So, together with journalist Richard Boston, he decided
> to set up a brewery based at Penrhos Court, a restaurant and hotel just
> outside Kington. At the time, the real ale offering in Herefordshire was
> poor. Most pubs were selling insipid brews. There were no breweries in
> Herefordshire, a sad state of affairs considering the huge volume of hops
> grown in the county.

Monty Python's Terry Jones (in red) at Penrhos Brewery, and a Penrhos Brewery beer mat

The then-owner of Penrhos, Martin Griffiths, remembers Terry visiting the restaurant from his nearby holiday cottage. Martin's partner, Daphne, was a pioneer in organic food, feeding their pigs on spent hops and curing meat with the beer. Penrhos Court gained a reputation, not just for food and beer, but for the stellar line-up of guests, a *Who's Who* of the early seventies' comedy and music scene: other Pythons (Michael Palin was at the brewery launch), Tubular Bell's Mike Oldfield and various members of Led Zeppelin. Martin:

> The writer Richard Boston was writing a weekly article about beer every Wednesday in *The Guardian* and that caught Terry's imagination and got him all enthusiastic about what beer should be. During a visit to our restaurant Terry said, "Look, I don't want to muscle in, but couldn't we start a brewery here?" He paid for the vessels, I plumbed them in and we made beer.

Speaking to Roy Plumley on the BBC's *Desert Island Discs* programme in 1983, Terry was asked about his Herefordshire brewery:

> It's wonderful. Well, when the beer's good it's wonderful, and when it's not, it isn't! The best thing about the brewery in a way is when I thought about setting it up in 1976, kind of nobody thought about doing anything like it for, I don't know, a hundred years or so (...) and since we set it up I think there's been something like 60 or 70 little breweries all over the country have sprung up.

Penrhos Brewery produced three core beers, including a Pale Ale known as *Jones's First Brew*. Sadly, the brewery was short-lived and closed in 1983. But it had made its mark.

Nick Davis of Hobsons Brewery in Cleobury Mortimer is another brewery to forge close links with hop growers, this time Geoff Thompson of Little Lambswick Farm, Eardiston, some seven miles from the brewery. When Geoff and his family stopped growing hops in 2018, Hobsons found a new supplier of British varieties of hops, Brook House Farm near Bromyard. Like all these breweries, the provenance of their beer ingredients is an important part of their story and marketing campaigns. Nick:

> For 25 years over 80% of the hops used by Hobsons Brewery were grown in the Teme Valley by Geoff, who would deliver our requirements direct from his kiln to ensure that the required bitterness and keeping-quality of each brew was covered. When Hobsons was growing and increasing its production of real ale, it was important to establish contracts with suppliers of raw ingredients, with a strong emphasis on forging long-lasting relationships to ensure quality hops and barley were readily available to us. It's important for us at Hobsons' brewers to work alongside hop growers to understand the varieties of hops and how they were growing and even often being on-site during the hop harvest in September.

Over the hills in nearby Leominster is a recent addition to brewing, Swan Brewery, run by beer aficionados, Gill Bullock and Jimmy Swan. Jimmy was former head brewer at Wye Valley. Their aim is to create beers with classic contours, and delicious depths, 'mellifluous maltiness, and heavenly hops'. They also nurture working relationships with hop growers and it has given them an understanding and appreciation of the expertise that goes into delivering hops to their brewery. Gill:

> We feel a part of the farming supply-chain, and much more connected. And from a marketing point of view, we have a better understanding of how hops are raised and can tell that story. A favourite occasion at Swan is brewing green hops during the picking season, fresh off the bine, sometimes still heavy with dew. It's particularly special. We agree

Leominster Priory curate, Reverend Matthew Burns (*left*) and Reverend Mike Kneen (*right*), both of the Leominster Ministry, sniffing hops at Swan Brewery (© Swan Brewery)

a few days before with the grower, so we know what hop variety we will be brewing. Within a few hours of them being picked they will be in the copper. It's our way of celebrating the hop harvest, and we invite a team from the Ministry at Leominster Priory for a service, reading a blessing of the wort, then a lunch of courgette soup grown in soil enriched with spent hops. And a glass of Herefordshire beer. It's a wonderful celebration.

It's not just beer – other uses of the hop

The hop's antiseptic and preservative qualities mean that it is in demand for uses other than just beer. Hildegard von Bingen, the noted German abbess, herbalist, composer and author (1098–1179), wrote that hops had little use for humans, noting that they 'increase melancholy in men,' yet adding, 'its bitterness fends off decomposition of beverages and increases shelf life'. She may have approved of some of these:

- Hop pillows are a traditional remedy for sleeplessness. George III was said to sleep on a bed of hop pillows to calm him.
- Hop pillows were also good for toothache and headache.
- Washing one's hair daily with a freshly-prepared hop tea helps prevent hair loss.
- Spent hops are used for plant food and even cattle feed.
- The stem of the hop can be pulped down for use in the paper and cardboard industry.
- A hop poultice is used to relieve stiffness and pain.
- When steeped as a tea, hops can aid indigestion.
- And, from a 1902 article, The Lord's Housemaid, 'linen covers displayed with a spray of the graceful hop, are attractive in appearance'.

Some brewers use experimental hop varieties in their recipes, usually identified with a number and not a name. When Jeanette Hills was working in the greenhouses at Claston, Peter Davies named experimental varieties after the women working there:

They sent them off to different breweries to try. The one named after me went off to Brains in Cardiff, but they never used it after. The only one still going is Pilot, which was initially named after my sister Ros. When my son Paul was making beer with his brewery Calpaul, they used Pilot hops unaware that they had been named after his Aunty Ros.

Chris Gooch and his team at Teme Valley Brewery, attached to The Talbot pub in Knightwick, were early pioneers in microbrewing and flag wavers for the area's hop growers. He is widely considered the gentleman of brewing. He is also a founder-member of Hopshires, highlighting the crucial role the hop-growing industry plays in the West Midlands for British brewing.

The Clift family at Lulsley Court, Worcestershire, former hop growers, had been running the pub for over 40 years. In 1997 Chris took on the roles of brewer, manager, quality control and sales manager. His philosophy has always been the same – local hops from the Midlands:

Chris Gooch of Teme Valley Brewery, at the bar of The Talbot (© M. O'Mahony)

To start with we only used hops from Lulsley Court, but then we needed some varieties they didn't grow, so we started to use hops grown in Herefordshire and Worcestershire. The key factors in our beers are always hop-forward, extraordinary-tasting beers. And in order to brew those beer styles you need traditional British hops. You can substitute hop varieties, but you don't get the same beer out. Even if you grow British hop varieties abroad you get a different profile of aroma and flavour out. So there's no doubt for small brewers one of the delights is that year after year hops express different characteristics. For us it was Fuggles, Goldings and Challenger. It may be something the public don't notice, but brewers do. For me it's a pleasure.

When the brewery first opened in 1997 it was the first year First Gold became commercially available, one of the first of the new hedgerow hop

(© Dan Barrett, Unsplash)

varieties. Then we used a lot of the newer varieties, especially Sovereign and Cascade, which was grown just 200 yards behind the brewery at Ankerdine Farm. Now it's grown by Mark Andrews at Ledbury. We used to have hopyards up to the back gate here at the Talbot. You could throw a cork out the back of the pub and hit one.

When I look at the growers now, they are all working at the peak of their expertise. No slack in there at all. They are all proactive. None of them are sticks in the mud and all are adopting new varieties. They've taken on the messages from merchants, growers and breeders that the future is innovation as well as traditional varieties. The other quality they share is that they are all stubborn. They have stuck with hop growing through a time which almost seemed pointless. And we are very lucky for that.

10

Hop Research & Development: the future

This is the centre of the hops trade. Not Kent. Herefordshire, Shropshire and Worcestershire, this is the stronghold and I would put that down to the entrepreneurial integrity of the farmers up here. We've always been developers, whether it was cattle with the Herefords bred for excellence, or with cider fruits, we do the same with the hops. Whatever we did, we wanted to do it better.

Peter Walker

P ETER Walker's great-grandfather was the epitome of the hop entrepreneur and innovator:

He put in a steam spraying system, pipes underneath all the hopyards, a big steam pump and a big collecting tank, where they stirred up all the sprayer. Pumped it out over the hopyard and there would be lances on hose pipes in every third row, and a gang of people would plug into a set of taps, the hooter would go, and they would all open up their guns and spray hops, ten-yards one way and ten-yards the other. Then the hooter would go off again and they'd disconnect and move on to another section. In the 1930s his grandsons actually motorised a mobile spraying unit to go behind a horse pulling a Model-T engine mounted on the back with a tank and a spray pump. They trained the horse to cope with the noise of the motor and took that up and down the fields.

It wasn't about saving labour so much. Most of it was trying to get a more consistent harvest because if you look at the figures before they started spraying hops, it went up and down like a yo-yo. Could have a blight year with two or three tons of hops, then a heavy year with 30 or 40 tons. Once they started spraying for blight, insects and aphids in particular, that tended to level out the actual cropping each year. For most people, damson was another crop. Around us it was planted in all the hedgerows as a crop; they didn't realise at the time that it was the alternative host for the hop aphid.

PESTS AND DISEASES

I have a friend who says 90% of his farm is cereals and 10% hops. But his effort and his interest is 90% on the hops and 10% on the cereal. Hops are a way of life and are fascinating and challenging. Whereas cereals are bread and butter and they don't reach highs, but they don't reach lows either. **Dr Peter Darby**

Pests and diseases are the scourge of the hop grower's life. Over the last 25 years there have been fewer and fewer crop protective products available to growers. Any work being done on fungicides and pesticides is for major crops, the cereals, rice and maize. It is frustrating and inhibiting for growers. Therefore, for now at least, their only recourse has been the ongoing in-house research by their peers in the hop industry. And this has succeeded in producing new hop varieties that are resistant to, or tolerant of, pests and diseases.

Dr Peter Darby is a retired hop researcher and public figurehead behind Wye Hops Ltd, a subsidiary of the British Hop Association and the vital research centre for the British Hop industry. He was at the front-line of hop research for over 40 years and understands the challenges and frustrations that British hop growers face. Investment in crop-protection products often comes down to simple economics and politics:

The pharmaceuticals are not doing research because hops are not such big customers. Virtually all the products that are being used for hops were initially developed for other crops and have been tried and happened to have been found to be effective. The hop isn't represented in many of the EU countries and so some of the products that are needed for hop growing have been banned by the EU on a majority from countries that don't grow them at all.

Then there are political matters like the recognition of pesticide limits between countries. American hops have completely different minimum requirements to some European hops for example. It is not a level playing field. We have often pointed out that brewers in this country are using Australian hops, for example, that are sprayed with compounds that can't be used here. So there is a lack of harmonisation globally, not just in the EU.

Another front-line hop worker is crop doctor Jonathan Blackman, an agronomist for H.L. Hutchinson Ltd. In the 1990s he worked on hop research at Rosemaund experimental farm (*see overleaf*). Today, hops are one of many crops he keeps an eye on, from diagnosing and advising on nutrition, to crop husbandry and soil health. The hop is, he says, a bigger challenge every year because there are fewer solutions in terms of crop protection:

> The hop is totally different from any other crop plant. It's a perennial that starts from nothing every year to being five or six-metres tall and an awful lot of foliage and biomass production by the time we have the harvest in early September. So from a crop protection point of view, it's a moving target. With hops you start to spray something that looks like the height of wheat crop. By the time of the last spray in August it's like a large cider apple tree. I can't think of any other crop that is like that. If you look in books on pests for apples, there are pages and pages that can potentially affect them. But in hops there are two main pests: the damson-hop aphid and the two-spotted spider mite, and our two main diseases are powdery mildew and downy mildew.
>
> Ever since hop growing started to expand from the end of the nineteenth century, the damson-hop aphid really has been the main pest problem. There's historic production information for hops in the UK and if you go back to before the insecticide era you will see a very clear biennial pattern, i.e. you get a good crop year and you get a bad one. But post-Second World War, there is a much smoother pattern of annual hop production as insecticides come into usage.

A DIRTY AND UNPLEASANT BUSINESS

Pest and disease control was a dirty and unpleasant business indeed and the grower's arsenal was a modest one. Sulphur, endured and cursed by hop dryers of old, was used in the mid-nineteenth century to help control mould and, until the end of the Second World War, aphids were controlled by dusting plants with nicotine powder distributed by horse-drawn powdering machine.

Some folk customs were employed alongside such innovations. Janet Parker's father had one, although the window of application was very limited indeed:

> During the growing season, the farmers practically lived in the hopyards to keep them free of disease. Dad used to get up at 3am to see if it was calm enough to powder the hops with sulphur. There was a particular tree, a black Poplar, and if the leaves were very still, he went ahead. But the leaves were rarely still enough!

Rosemaund Experimental Farm

Rosemaund Experimental Farm at Preston Wynne was a local centre for research on damson-hop aphid control in the 1980s, looking at foliar and soil-applied insecticides. George H. Edwards died in 1952. In the years following the First World War he was said to be the second largest grower in Herefordshire, with two farms, Livers Ocle and Rosemaund. At Rosemaund, he turned 150 acres of gorse land into hopyards, and his reputation for growing Fuggles in particular was considered second to none. His model farm Rosemaund was ideal for the Ministry of Agriculture, just then looking for suitable land for an experimental farm. They purchased it at auction for a price of £39,000, a Ministry spokesman explaining that:

> we will be investigating general farm problems, regarding crops, including hops and livestock on the Herefordshire type of soil – red sandstone. The Ministry is buying farms in various parts of the country for such a purpose and Rosemaund was selected because it was such a good hop farm. Up to the moment, research work in connection to hops had only been carried out in the south-east and it was well-known that soil and climate conditions in the west are very different.

The work on hops at Rosemaund came to an end in 1998 when the Ministry withdrew funding. Alumni included hop specialist Fred Dickens, hopyard builder; Geoff Godsell, who experimented with different types of trellis work there; agronomist Jonathan Blackman; and Peter Glendinning, who today manages the hop-breeding programme at Charles Faram.

Another piece of folk knowledge was handed down by Bert Francis, an old and reliable farm-hand, and demonstrated to Richard Phillips at Eggleton Court a very practical lesson in pest control:

> Bert taught me all sorts of things. When we were looking for insects he showed me that if you suspected red spider in a hopyard you should get a leaf, turn it over, get some dust off the soil, rub it into a finer dust, and then sprinkle it over the leaf. The dust showed where the cobwebs for the red spiders were. It works. I've taught my children that.

The most valuable part of the grower's armoury costs nothing at all, apart from sleepless nights: hyper-vigilance, trudging the yards day in, day out, looking, touching, examining. It never ends and could easily induce paranoia. It is something engrained in all growers. Philip Price at Thinghill Court:

> I was checking all the time for blight and disease. That was part of my job, to pull the bine down, have a look, see how much blight there was. If it had blight, then the sprayer was out. You had to be out all the time powdering hops with a tractor. Bordeaux was used to stop the mildew and I've still got a tin in my greenhouse now to stop the mould on my potatoes. We used to start about five in the morning, while the hops still had dew on so that it stuck, and then we'd finish and think, "thank god for that!" We would come in and the old man would say, "the sun's out now, we'll put some sulphur on". So back out again with this spraying machine and sulphur powder, little old tractors, no cabs, covered in dust. It was awful.

'PESTILENCE' HITS THE HOPYARD

New developments: further research into hop wilt will start in 1981 under the sponsorship of the Department of Hop Research at Wye College, paid for jointly by Messrs Guinness and the Hop Marketing Board. Hop Marketing Board magazine, May 1981

A menace that haunted growers in the latter half of the twentieth century was the dreaded verticillium wilt. Its gradual march across hop-growing districts brought some growers to their knees, while others accepted defeat. Official accounts first record wilt in its 'fluctuating form in 1924 in Kent, before developing its virulent progressive strain, with its menace to the industry, in about 1930.' (A.H. Burgess, *Hops, Botany, Cultivation and Utilization*, 1964). By 1947, the Minister for Agriculture made an order which required notification of any trace of the disease and 'the destruction of all dead and dying bines and leaves of hop plants on premises where the disease exists.'

It got the best of them and it seemed there was little anyone could do. Well-respected amongst his peers, Graham Andrews of Bosbury was meticulous in his approach and was a one-time mentor to Charles Pudge at Frogend:

> I was probably not the master of attention to detail like him but was always interested in how other people did things. He loved his hops, but the wilt got in there too. It was spreading, and we were talking one day, and he said, "if I get wilt …", and I said, "Graham, you've got that wrong. It will be when, not if". Two years later he got it. I think it was very difficult for him.

When Peter Davies of Claston, the self-styled hop king of Europe got wilt, there was a sense that this disease was unstoppable. The Conservative Association's 1975 barn dance at Claston, arranged to mark MP David Gibson-Watt's 18 years of service, was hastily rearranged when wilt made an unwelcome appearance. A pariah status fell on those afflicted. Before his farm was hit, Graham Andrews telephoned the chair of Ledbury National Farmers Union, the unflappable Brian Willder at Leighton Court, when news of Peter Davies' plight became known. Graham argued for the NFU to back the closure of the Hereford to Tarrington road, which ran past Peter's hopyards: 'He phoned me up on a Sunday morning at 7am and I had just got back from a Bob Dylan concert! He said we had better get the roads closed because otherwise they'll be bringing that infection up and down the road. I just said, we can't do that.'

Leighton Court fell victim too, bringing an end to decades, if not centuries, of hop growing there, and there were others with a similar history, who succumbed to the disease. Its appearance was shocking and the impact visceral. Brian:

> I had looked at some of these plants in the hopyard and didn't like it. But you don't want to face up to the truth, do you? And I was going around one day, and this lad said, "you know what this is, don't you? It's wilt". In

my heart of hearts I knew we weren't going to avoid it because it was all over the place. We liked to think wilt was a disease of the south-east and we wouldn't get it up here. But we did. It was pretty devastating, made you feel very sick. You want to try and pretend it's a bad dream, but you haven't got many hours to do that. Oh yes, fellow growers kept clear of you all right. It could be quite isolating.

Contract workers were blamed for bringing the disease onto some virus-hit farms via their spades, forks and boots. Peter Walker was like others and learnt to manage his worry, but the underlying fear was always there:

> I wouldn't go through Suckley to Ledbury, instead I'd go via Malvern, because you wouldn't want to go through the areas that had wilt. You could pick it up on your car tyres, into your yard, onto your shoes, walk it out around the hopyard. We were very careful about who we had our oil from too. We'd try and make sure they were from the other side of us, from Stourport for example, knowing their lorries, with luck, weren't going to Ledbury. But it was a death knell for some smaller enterprises.

The impact on growers' lives and the growing areas was largely missed by mainstream news media outlets and those outside farming communities. Yet the impact led to some life-changing and hard-headed decisions. Mike Skittery's family at Little Marcle didn't escape:

> We absolutely dreaded it. We worked hard but when we got it we couldn't control it. It was in the varieties that we could sell well too, that was the worst thing, the varieties the brewery wanted. So we grew a tolerant variety in the end, Target, but it just wasn't worth as much. In the end we ended up with just that variety because the others were riddled with the wilt. And that's really why we gave up in the end. It wasn't worth our while. It was a bit depressing when we got it, but it was inevitable. I think my brother and I made the final commitment to get out of hops because Father was getting on in years. He didn't want to get out because he was so enthusiastic, but it was something we had to do financially really. And that's the bottom line. It was difficult for Dad, but he could understand why it was happening. And in the end, it was a relief really.

A Handful of Hop Varieties

by Dr Peter Darby, hop researcher and the public figurehead for
Wye Hops Ltd, a subsidiary of the British Hop Association (retired)

Admiral (1996)

This variety was the highest alpha-acid variety yet bred in Britain. I needed a name which conveyed British, the top of the tree, and began with 'A'. This was because Ray Neve had been through the alphabet, ending with Saxon, Viking, Yeoman and Zenith. The HMB continued to ask for names to follow the alphabet and so I had to start again at 'A'. The only other name which met these criteria was Apex which sounded like a cheap airline.

Bramling Cross (1951)

This variety arose as a seedling from a cross between Bramling Golding and a male line derived from the wild Manitoban. The name was similar to saying "a seedling of Bramling".

Challenger (1972)

Ray Neve had several published aims and objectives. One such challenge was to combine good aroma with disease resistance. In this variety he had downy mildew resistance, powdery mildew resistance (although that was lost whilst the variety was still in farm trials) and good aroma. It had met his challenge.

First Gold (1996)

There was much debate about what to call this variety. It was the World's first dwarf variety. To link it to Goldings, Brewers Gold and similar names which linked our hop breeding with the best quality, we wanted to have 'Gold' in the name as well as conveying that it was the first of its kind. Ideas such as 'Golden First' were considered but 'First Gold' was eventually the chosen combination.

Fuggle (1875)

Named after Mr Richard Fuggle of Brenchley of Kent, who, between 1861 and 1875, introduced this variety to the British hop growers. It was "Mr Fuggle's hop", shortened to "Fuggles".

Goldings (1790)

Named after Mr William Golding of West Malling, Kent who about 1790 introduced this variety to the British hop growers. It was "Mr Golding's hop", shortened to "Goldings".

Pilgrim (2001)

I had been freed from the need to use the alphabet and so I chose this name for the variety bred to have the strongest resistance to wilt disease. It comes from the hymn and poem by John Bunyan ".... who against all disasters would soldier night and day to be a Pilgrim". It conveyed a variety which would fight the ravages of wilt disease.

Progress (1965)

This was the result of the co-operative breeding programme between East Malling Research and Wye College to breed a wilt resistant, Fuggle-type variety. It was considered that this was making progress.

Sovereign (2006)

I was again trying to link British aroma hops with enduring quality conveyed by "Gold", the initial thought of 'Gold Sovereign' got truncated to just 'Sovereign'.

Target (1972)

Ray Neve had several published aims and objectives. One such was to breed a wilt resistant high alpha-acid variety. This was his target and so he named the variety which first met his target.

WGV (1932)

This was a seedling of Bates Brewer, reputed to be a Golding found at the Whitbread Hop Farm, Beltring, Kent. Seedlings of Goldings were called Golding Varieties and, hence, it was Whitbread's Golding Variety.

Name of Hopyard	Kind of hop	Acreage	Total weight				Per Acre	Bushels	Per cwt	No. of Pockets
			T	cwt	qr	lb				
Pifers	Tolhursts	2¾	1	18	0	26	lb 4·27	3 4 5 4	9 1	2 5
Lower Hopyard	Colegate	2½	2	6	3	7	17·26	4 5 0 0	9 8	3 0
Wirework, short length	Fuggle	2½		17	3	14	7·1	1 5 6 8	8 7	1 1
Lower Hopyard	Bobb	2½	1	17	0	13	14·84	3 6 8 0	9 9	2 4
Ling Croft	Bobb	3	1	12	2	19	10·89	2 7 9 2	8 6	2 0
Ling Croft	Mathons	4½		17	2	10	4·40	1 4 9 6	8 5	1 1
Lower Hopyard	young Fuggles	3	1	8	2	9	9·23			1 8
Lower Hopyard	(Neil's) Fuggle	3	2	4	1	5	14·76			2 7
Lower Hopyard	Fuggles	1½	1	5	1	2	16·68			1 6
		24³⁄₇	13	8	1	21	12·13			1 8 2

Hop varieties listed on a ledger for Ankerdine Farm (© Peter Walker)

Meeting the appetite for new beer flavours has been driving hop research in the last half a century. The US West Coast microbreweries have led the way in creating beers where the character of hops – piney, floral, grapefruit – take centre stage. These flavours, however, are not the range traditional English hop varieties can produce. To compete with them, the breeding programmes are developing new varieties producing similar flavours from our unique terroir and maritime climate. They said it could not be done. It has now.

The entry of the UK into the EEC prompted British brewers to demand that their future purchases should be related to world market prices (and not just the domestic one). At the same time, brewers changed their requirements from the traditional varieties of Fuggles and Goldings to a greater quantity of high alpha hops. It was fortunate for the English grower that the hop-breeding programme at Wye College was able to produce a succession of high alpha varieties suitable for English production, meeting the demands of the home market as well as providing a competitive product for the export market.

The hop-breeding programme in the UK has a long pedigree. Its foundations were laid by Professor Ernest Salmon in 1906 at Wye College. He is considered by some as a pioneer in looking to wild hop plants as the source of new hop characters. Under his tenure, some of the most famous and widely-grown hops in the world were developed. Salmon aimed to produce hops with a high resin content. He also introduced American hops, with their punchy, citrusy flavours, into the breeding programme. It was a wise move. These flavours are what the market is demanding today. His successors, Ray Neve and, most recently, Peter Darby, have continued his work, pushing research even further and developing disease-resistant and -tolerant varieties, alongside new ranges of flavours. In 2006, the withdrawal of funding from DEFRA closed Wye College. The hop research department's head, Peter Darby, teamed up with renowned Kent hop grower Tony Redsell OBE, to form Wye Hops Ltd, in order to continue a research programme. As it is a subsidiary of the British Hop Association, it has become a vital research centre for the British hop industry. The project is funded largely by the British Hop Association growers.

Peter Darby's training was in genetics and pathology and so he fitted the bill very well when Wye College was looking for a pathologist for its plant breeding programme. He is fascinated by the hop:

It is the tallest temperate crop that there is, growing up to 15- to 18-feet high. It is the tallest plant that is grown commercially. The plant itself produces the female and not the male plant, and the female produces cones, which are basically modified flowers. And it is these that are used in the brewing process. None of the leaves or bine are used, or actually the cones themselves, but rather the secondary product, the glands. They contain the resins and essential oils.

The principal thing in modern brewing is that flavour and aroma come from these essential oils and the bitterness comes from the resins in the hop cones. And so part of the principles of breeding for these characteristics is either to have very specific oils that give a very distinctive flavour, or to have a higher content of resin to give more bitterness. So our primary aim is for the brewer. But then that's no use if the grower can't grow the crop, so the secondary objectives are for agronomy – for yield, productivity, resistance to pests and diseases and so on. So you are breeding for the brewer and the grower and of course for the environment, trying to reduce the use of pesticides to increase biodiversity and all of that side of things as well.

Peter has succeeded in breeding more than a dozen new hop varieties in this country, among them Admiral, First Gold, Herald, Phoenix, Pilgrim, Diva, Sovereign, Merlin and Boadicea. He hails the last in this list, Boadicea, as one of his proudest achievements:

She is the first variety to be resistant to the hop aphid and to be grown without being sprayed for aphids. She was called Boadicea for obvious reasons, a warrior, the Iceni queen, who fought off the invading Romans and so, hop-wise, fought off the invasion of aphids. All hops are female, and it had to be a queen fighting off the invaders. And that's what she does. And another is Pilgrim, so named because of the hymn. We used to sing John Bunyon's *He who would valiant be*, he who is valiant against all disaster, and Pilgrim is the variety that could withstand the disaster of the hop wilt. And we have others that have names that are only on trial at the moment. Boadicea is used a lot by Adams brewery, and Phoenix by Carlsberg.

When Wye Hops Ltd formed in 2006, with the British Hop Association (BHA), their principal aim was to save the historic hop collection that had been curated over decades of research. Britain's collection of historic hops, previously held at Wye College, is now principally in the care of renowned hop farmer Tony Redsell OBE, at China Farm in Kent. The site was selected mainly due to wilt-free conditions. In 2010 it was awarded the status of The National Hop Collection and becoming officially part of the nation's plant heritage. This collection can sometimes spring surprises. A hop called Ernest is enjoying new-found popularity with brewers after nearly a century languishing in the vaults. Peter takes up the story:

> Ernest was a seedling collected in 1921 and it was so unremarkable that Professor Ernest Salmon wrote a note explaining that he planted it in 1923. That's all. He didn't make another single note on it until 1939, when he wrote: "powerful, definitely American, fruity flavours, not in any way commercial". But these powerful American flavours were definitely not what was wanted then. So it rested there for nearly 20 years until 1953 when it was tested for resistance to wilt and Ernest was found to be resistant. Therefore, in 1956 it went to farm trials. But in 1959 Salmon died and his successor Ray Neve was getting rid of everything, he wanted a clean slate, and wasn't keen to take on anything that was an also-ran in Salmon's books. But, because it was on farm trials, it was scheduled for brewing trials in 1959, but it failed then because it was so American. So when I reviewed what we were going to take from Wye Hops into this collection in 2006, I rejected it. So it was dead. Salmon rejected it, Ray Neve rejected it and I rejected it.
>
> But when we got here and laid stuff out we realised we had slightly more space than we thought, so I put in six of the varieties I had rejected. And that was one of them. And because it was added late it was right on the end of a row, which is where we stop to talk to visitors. And one day four different visiting groups said, "hey, this one is interesting". And we did some trial brews and it was giving flavours microbreweries are now looking for, these powerful, fruity American flavours. Almost to the word, exactly what Salmon had written down. And it's what is wanted now. It was named Ernest after Ernest Salmon.

Charles Faram's Malvern base is home to another hop-breeding programme, run under the expert eye of Peter Glendinning. Some West Midlands growers are being co-opted into the programme, growing trial varieties, and some brewers too, producing beers from these new breeds. Ledbury Real Ales has brewed several experimental ales from the Charles Faram programme. So new are the varieties they are yet to have names and at this early stage they merely have code numbers. First they have to be proven to be viable. There are reasons to be optimistic. Will Rogers is Group Technical Director:

As a commercial breeding programme, we can share the risk with growers. What we have seen, not just in the short term but also in the long term, is a movement towards more flavoursome hops, more American. We describe it as New World hop flavours. So customers' tastes are moving towards that. I don't think that's a trend that's going to go away. There will be a market for big citrusy, tropical fruit characteristics and we were looking for those flavours from British hops. Ten years ago we were told that was impossible with our maritime climate, but we think we're just about there. Harlequin is at the advanced farm trial stage and we are very excited about that. In a blind tasting, no one even considered it might be from the UK and we consider that to be a big success.

We help brewers develop recipes all the time. If they give us what they would like to achieve we will try to help them achieve it. Swan Brewery for instance have used Ernest in one of their brews. My favourite hop is Jester because it's one of our new varieties and it is also a great grower's hop because it's fantastically disease resistant. When I started here in 2008 we were told you couldn't achieve these big citrusy flavours in a hop in the UK. So Peter Glendinning made some crosses with Cascade and a couple of years later we got a seedling and cone from the first plant. Peter took some of the cones, dried them and put them into a little pot. He brought them in to show me and Paul (Corbett, Charles Faram's Managing Director) and when we smelt them we were completely taken aback. We'd been told that it was impossible and yet here we had a hop that had those America characteristics in a UK hop. Paul thought Peter was joking and that's where Jester gets its name. We proved a little company in the middle of Worcestershire could produce something really world class.

THE DWARF HOP

The most significant development in hop growing in recent decades has been the introduction of the dwarf variety. Peter Davies

From the early 1990s, dwarf hop varieties such as First Gold, Herald and Pioneer, started to make appearances in the region's hopyards. The dwarf hop was seen as the development that would drag growers into the twenty-first century. It hasn't quite worked out that way. Taking down existing hopyards and replacing them with the hedgerow-type varieties, is hideously expensive. But it has been a good move for some growers. Advantages include lower capital costs for investment, the erection of cheaper trellis work, and lower recurrent costs, particularly labour (a dwarf hop harvest can operate on a quarter of the labour of the conventional hop, particularly at harvest time). There are also environmental advantages (biological control is more of a possibility on the dwarf variety); and simplified training and husbandry. It is, said dwarf hop grower Charles Pudge, 'a no brainer. You plant them, spray them and harvest them. It opens it up to less specialism. You don't have to string them; it's basically fencing technology.'

Dwarf hop harvester (© Mervyn Carless)

Peter Davies was an innovator, but, for the introduction of the dwarf hop variety to this country, he shared the crown with others, all elder statesmen in the industry. The key figure was Ray Neve of Wye College. In 1911 his predecessor Ernest Salmon made a note in his records (he was, like all the scientists, a prodigious note-taker) describing two dwarf hop plants. They were described thus: 'hops densely clustered, very fruitful, of no direct promise.' That would have been the end of this particular story were it not for Neve. In 1977 he went to the USA for a scientific commission of hop growers. While there, they were shown a demonstration of varieties growing on low trellis, up to around six feet high. It was a complete failure. On his return journey Neve began to ruminate on the idea that this system could work in the UK. And he quickly identified the issue: the Americans were growing the wrong varieties. Peter Darby:

It was believed if we could breed a variety to suit that system that would be the answer. Neve came back and walked into the hop-garden the following morning and saw immediately a plant that fitted the

Dwarf hop harvester at work at Tedney (© Peter Walker)

bill, of dwarf stature and realised that he'd seen them throughout his career, since he started in 1953. Suddenly he saw their potential, so he immediately selected some hop seed off this plant and from that seed the whole programme developed. He then discussed the idea with other growers. John Knott and Peter Davies both claimed it was their idea, but it wasn't; it was Ray Neve's. They had the idea but not the key feature, the right variety. So Neve pollinated the seed in 1977, grew it, selected out the dwarves, grew them and they were ready for their very first assessment in 1981. So that's when I came in and my first harvest job was to pick these dwarf varieties and see if they were economically viable or not, if there was a yield there. I took it over in 1982, and the crosses I made in 1984 led to the first dwarf varieties, Pioneer and Harold.

Dwarf hops account for around 23% of the UK acreage. They are located, for the most part, here in the West Midlands, largely because of historical and socio-economic reasons. The area was considered underdeveloped; therefore, grants were made available to purchase the expensive and specialised machinery, developed from a blackcurrant picker, this was integral to the dwarf hop harvest. These funding openings presented attractive possibilities to growers who had persevered despite all the hop could throw at them.

John Walker at Tedney, Winterbourne, grows ordinary and organic dwarf hop varieties (Sue Okell near Bosbury is another organic hop grower). His organic hops are used in the Duchy Organic Beer brand. His farm straddles the Herefordshire–Worcestershire border, helping him separate the two crops. The Walker family are a well-known family in the hop-growing world. John, however, didn't start growing his crop until the early 1990s:

When we started, we were looking for something that was going to give us an income really. It was quite an undertaking but we had the advantage of being able to share my cousin's kilns and machines. We went into dwarfs and have been growing them ever since. We sought advice at the time when deciding on dwarf varieties. The tall varieties at the time were still susceptible to wilt and the dwarf seemed a cheaper and easier way for people like us who didn't really know about what we were doing! Peter Davies at Claston was one of the reasons I went into dwarf varieties. He was an enthusiast for them and he came here and helped us set up.

The structure is simpler, more like fencing. We started erecting the yards ourselves and soon realised we weren't going to do it properly so soon got people in who knew what they were doing, including Mervyn Carless. A dwarf hopyard is cheaper to set up but then your yields are about two thirds of the taller crop. So everything is cheaper. I'm not sure if the growing bills are cheaper but the labour bill is cheaper and it's easier to set up. So as a newcomer, it was easier to get into.

Charles Pudge was another enthusiast. He also grows dwarf hops, but he's suffered to get to this point; we've established that hop growing is not for the faint-hearted, and Charles epitomises that. He has ten generations of growers behind him – 'it's a phenomenal legacy, or it shows how dull we are!' – but his humour and indomitability may have seen him through the tough times:

We had tall hops, but the wilt started in 1988, took about eight years to destroy the whole lot, then they all went. It was all good wirework and I thought it was rather sad. We decided when the wilt was getting bad, in about 1995, we would plant apples too and decided to plant a hundred acres of dwarf hops here then. There would have been six or eight other growers got into them then. It depended how fast the wilt had been spreading on farms. When wilt came through there were generations of hop growers, 40 or 50, who suddenly realised corn-growing was a lot easier. So when it all went wrong they decided to give it up. But I think it's in the blood – that's why we keep going. I love hops.

That was one of the reasons I went into dwarf hops because all the infrastructure was already here. I'd only known the tall variety, so I had to learn another way of growing them. My father grew only Fuggles for 40 years and even then he said that wasn't long enough to understand the hop plant. He tried a couple of different varieties, but he didn't like them and went back to Fuggles. Well I've learned two different systems and 25 varieties. Now I grow First Gold and Endeavour. The growing system is obviously different; we don't have as much casual labour about nowadays, but you still get the smell when we're picking.

Harvesting and development of the new dwarf hop varieties also required innovation of an engineering kind: a mobile picking machine. The combined experiences of a designer, grower and engineer came together, Robin Peers, Edward Thompson (Pixley Court) and Robert Chapman (Bavenhill Engineering), and the 'Robin', was born, the prototype dwarf hop machine. Robin Peers:

> CWF was a small subcontractor to the local engineering companies and it did not have its own product. One of our directors was a hop farmer, and we purchased the hop interests of Bruff in 1978. We planned to make spare parts for Bruff machines and provide services – in those days there were still probably around 80 individual hop growers in the West Midlands – and recruited some Bruff staff.
>
> In about 1980, we were invited to build a completely new two-machine set-up for harvesting and drying for Allied Breweries at Brierley Court. This was a big job for us, we enlarged our Callow Hill factory and recruited several more ex-Bruff staff, including Lawrence Lloyd and Peter Cale, without whose help we would have struggled. We also got orders from Australia for two Super E machines. But by 1985, the industry was shrinking fast and the directors decided to sell up and close the factory.
>
> In 1988 I joined forces with Edward Thompson and Robert Chapman of Bavenhill Engineering of Preston Cross. We purchased the remnants of Pattenden Machinery of Kent. They had made many blackcurrant harvesters and a few for raspberries. Edward was and is a substantial grower of blackcurrants, and in those days, also grew conventional hops.
>
> Wye College in Kent knew they would need a machine to harvest their trial plots of dwarf hops and built one in 1983 and again in 1989. Several growers were interested in these new varieties, and a limited supply of setts were allocated to a few. The prospect of much simpler wirework and reduced harvesting costs made possible by a mobile harvester was appealing (to some!)
>
> Peter Davies of Dormington as well as Edward Thompson of Pixley and others were keen to get setts, plant up and get us to make and supply a dwarf hop picker. So, we at Pattenden, felt there was a market for a machine and managed to get a DTI grant. This enabled us to purchase the Wye prototype, modify it to pick 8ft bines and trial it for a season.

In 1992, we set out the specification for the Peter Davies machine. I was chief engineer and did all the drawing and specifications. It was built at Bavenhill and harvested the 1994 crop. We had an amazing email from Peter Davies at the end of the first day's picking to congratulate us on producing a machine that performed perfectly without breaking down – a rare letter to receive from a farmer!

Pattenden was accustomed to give their machines the name of a bird. The dwarf hop picker was called Robin. It was my last project.

THE FUTURE

I think the future for hops is good. I don't feel part of a dying breed. A few years ago I was thinking of giving up and now my son is showing enthusiasm, so I'm starting to grow some more now. Hops are hard not to love. It's in the blood, that's why we keep going. **Charles Pudge**

Hop growing in the West Midlands is unquestionably smaller than at any other time in its history, but it is tighter and more streamlined than it has ever been too, and set to make an impact on world trade. The UK produces around 1.6% of the world hop production. It is tiny and that makes the British hop industry niche in the world market, but niche can be a great place to be. Exciting developments in peer-led research mean English hop growers are starting to compete with other countries and are producing flavour spectrums never thought possible here before.

There are, however, other hurdles to be overcome. The UK's vote to leave the EU in 2017 saw a sharp decline in the number of seasonal workers. This temporary influx of people, like the hand-pickers of old, remains crucial to the hop harvest. British farming and horticulture need around 80,000 workers every year, 99% of them from countries within the EU. How harvests will be staffed in future years remains uncertain, and that is an unsettling position for growers. The government expanded its pilot Seasonal Agricultural Workers Scheme (SAWS) to 10,000 in 2020 but there is no guarantee of similar initiatives in the years to come.

Instone Court's Simon Parker and his peers fill the shoes of the old guard who have passed away in recent years. Simon grows hops in the same fields his great-grandfather did and epitomises the mindset of the region's remaining growers:

There's certainly been times where, if we were sensible and economic, we would probably have got out of it. But because we love the crop so much that is why we have stuck at it. I think there is probably blinded love as much as anything when it comes to growing the hop.

This book has been a celebration of growers like Simon, past and present, the pickers and the industry, their stoicism and bloody-mindedness in the face of hostile markets, changing consumer tastes, pandemics, environments, weather and even the hop itself at times. Therein lies the enigma and the wonder of this crop. Long may hops continue to grow here.

At the end of the hop-picking season in 1956, a Dilwyn picker shared her thoughts with the local paper. It's an apt way to end the book:

> *In the warm September sunshine, picking hops can be such fun,*
> *Cracking jokes, exchanging gossip,*
> *And cribbing the unwary ones.*
>
> *Even when strong winds are blowing, and the rain comes pelting down,*
> *Seated 'neath an old umbrella, some plucky pickers carry on.*
>
> *Once again, the season's ended, no more we hurry to catch the bus,*
> *To take us to the Firs at Dilwyn,*
> *Where we helped to pick the hops.*
>
> *Cheerio fellow pickers, Dick and John and all the rest.*
> *Let's hope to meet again next season,*
> *Meanwhile I wish you all the best.*

GLOSSARY

Bagging hole hole in the floor of the kiln building, from which the *hop pocket* is suspended, and through which dried hops are pushed into the pocket (either by mechanical press, or previously by treading – thus *treading hole*)

Bagging hook metal handle with two curved hooks, used for gaining purchase on a *hop pocket*, to help with handling

Bait break-time food

Bine twining stalk of a hop plant

Booker person who kept a record of how many hops were picked by each picker (the *booker* and *busheller* generally worked together)

Burr flower of the hop

Bushel measure equal to 8 gallons/ 36 litres

Bushel basket basket used to measure the *bushels* of hops scooped from *cribs*

Busheller person responsible for counting the *bushels* picked into each *crib*

Coir string up which hops are trained in a *hopyard*, made from coconut fibres

Cowl vent at the top of the *hop kiln*, to allow moisture to escape during drying

Crib *hopyard* container into which hops were picked in the days of hand-picking, generally comprising sacking or canvas slung within a wooden frame

Cribbing practice of pushing a man or woman into a crib, and stealing a kiss

Crow's nest detachable metal frame attached to the back of the trailer in the *hopyard*, to provide a platform from which a hop picker could cut the *bines*

Flags remnants of hop plants (leaves and *bines*) still attached to the *wirework* in a *hopyard* after the *bines* have been cut down

Ganger person responsible for recruiting or overseeing hop pickers

Green sack hessian sacks used for transporting undried hops to the *kiln*

Green stage adjacent to the *kiln*, where *green sacks* are collected prior to drying

Hooker tool used for attaching hooks to the *wirework* in a *hopyard*

Hop barracks purpose-built accommodation for hop pickers

Hop devil open-sided metal brazier for heating and cooking

Hop factor dealer in hops, liaising between the growers and breweries

Hop kiln building for drying hops ('oast' or 'oasthouse' is used in Kent)

Hop pocket/ pocket large sack (typically around 6ft long) into which kiln-dried hops are pressed prior to the hops being marketed and sold

Hop press mechanical apparatus used to compress hops into the *pocket*

Hop token coin-like form of currency used on hop farms to denote the number of bushels picked, or the amount earned by the picker, to be cashed in later

Hop tyer person responsible for stringing the *hopyard* for the new season

Hopyard/ yard the field, with its poles and *wirework*, in which hops are grown (called a 'hop garden' in Kent)

Hop wilt disease affecting hops (*verticillium wilt*)

Kerf spade-shaped hoe

Kiln hair woven mat (traditionally of horse hair) or netting, laid over the open slats of the *kiln* floor, so hot air can pass through the hops evenly layered on top

Kiln man person responsible for overseeing the drying of the hops in a *kiln*

Monkey long wooden pole used by the *hop tyer* to guide the *coir* between the pegs in the ground and the hooks above when stringing a *hopyard*

Pole pitcher person responsible for erecting hop poles

Pole puller originally, person responsible for pulling the hop poles out of the ground so that the hops could be hand-picked from the *bine* into a *crib*

Sampler's tool bespoke scissored, clamping tool designed to remove a 'bite' of dried hops from a cut-open *pocket*, to enable a sample of hops to be assessed

Scratting hand-picking or plucking hops from a cut *bine*

Scuppet large-bladed shovel for pushing and moving hops in a *hop kiln* (the blade could be made of wood, or canvas stretched over a frame)

Spray side shoot from which the hops themselves sprout

Strig stem of a hop

Tallet hay loft

Tally-man person responsible for keeping a record of the hops picked by each picker, by using a *tally-stick*

Tally-stick length of stick, scored with a series of horizontal marks to indicate the number of *bushels* picked, then split lengthways, so that both the *tally-man* and the picker had a matching record of the *bushels* picked by that picker

Top-hook hook fixed to the *wirework*, over which the hop string is looped

Treading hole *see bagging hole*

Twiggling (or twiddling) stick stick used to coax hop shoots to begin to twine around a string in a clockwise direction

Vardo traditional horse-drawn living wagon used by Romany Gypsies, often elaborately decorated

Wagoner essentially the driver of a horse-drawn wagon; however, the wagoner could be a high-status worker on a farm, with a range of other responsibilities

Wirework framework of permanent wires supported on posts in a *hopyard*, and supporting the hop-bearing *coir* strings. Replaced hop poles

BIBLIOGRAPHY

Bennett, Judith M., *Ale, Beer and Brewsters in England: Women's work in a changing world 1300–1600,* Oxford University Press, 1996

Bromyard & District Local History Society, *A Pocketful of Hops,* Bromyard & District Local History Society, 2007

Brown, P., *Miracle Brew: Hops, Barley, Water, Yeast and the nature of beer,* 2017

Burgess, A.H., *Hops, Botany, Cultivation and Utilization,* Leonard Hill Books, 1964

Cashmore, M., *A Feast of Memories,* Westwood Press Publications, 1986

Clinch, G., *English Hops,* McCorquodale & Co. Ltd, 1919

Cordle, C., *Out of the Hay and into the Hop,* University of Hertfordshire Press, 2011

Davies, J., *Tales of Old Gypsies,* David & Charles, 1999

Davies, P., *A Herefordshire Tale, Claston, Hops and the Davies Family,* Logaston Press, 2007

Duncumb, J., *Words Used in Herefordshire,* 1804

Edlin, H.L., *Man and Plants,* Aldus Books, 1967

Faulkner, C., *Hops and Hop-pickers,* Faulkner Publications, 1992

Filmer, R., *Hops and Hop Picking,* Shire Publications Ltd, 1982

Fletcher, H.L.V., *Herefordshire,* Robert Hale Ltd, 1948

Geoghegan, R., *Apple Water: Povel Panni,* Hedgehog Poetry Press, 2018

Green, J., *Changing Scenes, Celebrating 150 years of the Tenbury Agricultural Society,* Tenbury Agricultural Society, 2008

Haggard, A., *Dialect and Local Usages of Herefordshire,* Grower Books, 1972

Havergal, F.T., *Herefordshire Words & Phrases,* W. Henry Robinson, 1887

Helme, J., *Hops'n'Hoptons, a History of Canon Frome, Herefordshire,* 2001

Herefordshire Federation of Women's Institutes, *Herefordshire Within Living Memory,* Countryside Books, 1993

Herefordshire Hop Kilns: An Introduction to these Unique Farm Buildings, GHAL Productions, 2004

Hunt, W.M., *Cradley, a Village History,* W.M. Hunt & Cradley Village Hall Committee, 2004

Ile Currie, J., *Three Centuries of a Herefordshire Village,* Owlstone Press, 2009

Lawrence, M., *The Encircling Hop: A History of Hops and Brewing,* Sawd Publications, 1990

Leather, Ella Mary, *The Folk-lore of Herefordshire,* Logaston Press, 2018

Luff, William, *In the Hop Fields,* Bretheren Archive

Macklin, J., *Bishopstone & Bunshill*, John Macklin Publications, 2011

Marden History Society, *The Oral History of the Parish of Marden*, 2008

Marshall, W., *Review and Abstract of the County Reports to the Board of Agriculture*, Augustus M. Kelley Publishers, 1968

Memories of Stoke Lacy 1952–2002

Moore, J., *September Moon*, William Collins, Sons & Co. Ltd, 1958

Neville Havins, P., *Portrait of Worcestershire*, Robert Hale & Company, 1974

Palmer, Roy, *The Folklore of the Black Country*, Logaston Press, 2007

— *The Folklore of Herefordshire & Worcestershire*, Logaston Press, 1992

Peers, R., *A Chapter in an Engineer's Life*, Aspect Design, 2019

Putman, R., *Beers and Breweries of Britain*, Shire Publications Ltd, 2004

Raven, M., *A Guide to Herefordshire*, Michael Raven, 1996

— *The Ross Workhouse Songbook*, Michael Raven, 1996

Rider Haggard, H., *Rural England Volume 1*, Elibron Classics, 2005

Robinson, G.M., *Agricultural Change: Geographical Studies of British Agriculture*, North British, 1988

Rogers, J.E. & A.G., *A History of Agriculture and Prices in England*, Nabu Press, 2011

Sandford, Jeremy, *Songs from the Roadside: 100 years of Gypsy Music*, Redlake Press, 1995

Scot, Reginald, *A Perfite Platforme of a Hoppe Garden*, Henrie Denham, 1576

Sinclair, T.R. & C.J., *Bread, Beer & the Seeds of Change*, CABI, 2010

Sturt, George, *A Small Boy in the Sixties*, The Harvester Press, 1977

Suckley Local History Society, *Aspects of Suckley*, Castle Hill Books, 2006

Tenbury & District Civic & Historical Society, *Tenbury and the Teme Valley: People and Places*, Logaston Press, 2007

Transactions of the Woolhope Naturalists' Field Club (various), WNFC

Trumpet Ploughing Society, *In the Wake of the Plough*, 2007

Weale, J., *A History of Bredenbury & its Landed Estate*, Bromyard & District Historical Society, 1997

West Midlands Group, *English County, A Planning Survey of Herefordshire*, Faber and Faber, 1946

Williams, P., *The Three Stanfords: A History of Stanford Bishop, Stanford Falcon and Stanford Regis*, Bromyard & District Local History Society, 2006

— *Whitbourne, A Bishops's Manor*, Orphans Press Ltd, 1979

INDEX